European Mennonite Voluntary Service, 1948-1972

European Mennonite Voluntary Service

Youth Idealism in Post-World War II Europe

CALVIN WALL REDEKOP

Foreword by Robert Lee

Publishing House
Telford, Pennsylvania

copublished with
Herald Press
Scottdale, Pennsylvania

Cascadia Publishing House LLC orders, information, reprint permissions:
contact@cascadiapublishinghouse.com
1-215-723-9125
126 Klingerman Road, Telford PA 18969
www.CascadiaPublishingHouse.com

European Mennonite Voluntary Service
Copyright © 2010 by Cascadia Publishing House
a division of Cascadia Publishing House LLC, Telford, PA 18969
Library of Congress Catalog Number: 2010022874
ISBN 13: 978-1-931038-79-9; **ISBN 10:** 1-931038-79-1
Book design by Cascadia Publishing House
"The loved and well-known MVS symbol: p. 1
Photos not otherwise credited are by the author.
Cover design by Merrill. R. Miller

The paper used in this publication is recycled and meets the
minimum requirements of American National Standard for Information Sci-
ences—Permanence of Paper for Printed Library Materials, ANSI Z39.48-1984.

Unless indicated otherwise, all Bible quotations are used by permission, all
rights reserved, and are from *The New English Bible*, The Delegates of the Oxford
University Press and the Syndics of the Cambridge University Press 1961, 1970.
Reprinted with permission.

Library of Congress Cataloguing-in-Publication Data
Redekop, Calvin Wall, 1925-
European Mennonite Voluntary Service : youth idealism in post-World War II
Europe / Calvin Wall Redekop ; foreword by Robert Lee.
p. cm.
Summary: "This book tells the story of the Mennonite-related work camp
movement and its efforts to organize volunteers to help reconstruct Europe
after World War II." "[summary]"--Provided by publisher.
Includes bibliographical references (p.   ) and index.
ISBN-13: 978-1-931038-79-9 (5.5 x 8.5" trade pbk. : alk. paper)
ISBN-10: 1-931038-79-1 (5.5 x 8.5" trade pbk. : alk. paper)
1. Mennonite Voluntary Service--History. 2. Reconstruction (1939-1951)--Eu-
rope 3. World War, 1939-1945--Mennonites. 4. Mennonites--Europe--History--
20th century. I. Title.

D810.C665R43 2010
940.53'144--dc22

2010022874

17 16 15 13 12 11 10   10 9 8 7 6 5 4 3 2 1

To the many thousands of young people who by their idealism, enthusiasm, and love contributed to the material and moral recovery of Europe after World War II. They also helped give birth to Mennonite Voluntary Service and the services it performed 1950-1972. Several organizations which emerged from MVS are still in operation and contributing in Europe and elsewhere.

The achievements of these many young people in the various camps are evident in the pages that follow. The impact of their lives in post-camp days on their communities, wherever they scattered, is also undoubtedly significant. I often dream of a mega-camper reunion at which campers could tell their "camping" stories and the contributions they subsequently made; maybe this book can become a surrogate reunion. The photos, though of necessity highly selective, will hopefully reinvigorate memory of those "happy days." This story is a testimony to their service.

The loved and well-known MVS symbol

CONTENTS

Foreword by Robert Lee   9

Author's Preface   12

Chapter 1: The Forerunners of MVS Work in Europe   • 19

Chapter 2: The Continued Development of European
Voluntary Service   • 29

Chapter 3: The Expansion/Diversification of
Mennonite Voluntary Service   • 53

Chapter 4: The History and Formation of
Mennonite Voluntary Service   • 63

Chapter 5: The Transformation/Termination of MVS   • 79

Chapter 6: The Context and the Vision   • 95

Table 1. Tabulation of International Work Camps   105

Table 2. MVS Volunteers from Following Countries   106

Table 3. Number of Work Camps and Participants   107

*Appendix 1. Account of Organizational Meeting of Mennonite
Voluntary Service*   108

*Appendix 2. Voluntary Service Responses in Post-World War II
Europe: A Timelinee*   110

Notes   112

Bibliography   125

The Index   128

The Author   132

FOREWORD

I am grateful for Cal Redekop's little book, *European Mennonite Voluntary Service*, especially since I was an early participant in the formation of this program but until now did not know what took place after we both left Europe, Cal in 1952 and I in 1953. Indeed I wish that I had been able to read this instructive book in my later work for Mennonite Central Committee (MCC) in Korea (1953-56) and under the Mennonite Mission Network as a missionary in Japan, beginning in 1959.

In this book Redekop narrates a slice of the history of the Mennonite Central Committee relief and refugee resettlement work in Europe after WWII that perhaps has been overshadowed by a sister program—the MCC Pax program (earlier narrated in *The Pax Story: Service in the Name of Christ, 1951-1976*, also by Redekop) that sent more than 1,100 North American young men to Europe and later elsewhere in refugee resettlement programs. In fact, Redekop was the European director of both programs in their formative stages.

In this second book Redekop, a trained sociologist and a participant-observer, provides a critical historical analysis of the innovative service of the young MCC volunteer "relief workers" who, serving "in the name of Christ" (the MCC motto), created a European Mennonite international workcamp program (MVS or MFD, in German *Mennonitischen Frei-*

9

willingendienstes), not only as an expression of their discipleship but also as a witness to their faith.

At the end of World War II the international work-camp movement brought diverse groups of idealistic young people and refugees together in physical labor to meet the material needs of recent enemies as a way to foster peace and reconciliation among both the war victims and offenders. These MFD/MVS Christian work camps included Bible study and worship to add a spiritual dimension to the healing process. During each work camp, a clear pattern emerged: the creation (birth) of community out of a diverse, often alienated group of individuals who through daily labor, discussion, study, and worship would form a new community, encounter conflict and (often dramatically) find reconciliation, and in the end depart in a fond farewell (death) scene.

Thus the work camp experience became a transformative (or conversion) experience, a paradigm of a new way of life for many when they returned to their everyday life. Hence, from the beginning, the MVS vision was more than emergency relief and rehabilitation (e.g., refugee housing); it was also *development*, here a holistic ministry of the spiritual renewal and unity of our European counterparts, the Dutch, German, Swiss and French Mennonites.

Redekop provides a fine-grained analysis of the rapid expansion of MVS-MFD and its sudden demise or "transmogrification." In general terms he explains the consequences of the lack of differentiation between the emergency relief, rehabilitation, and the further goal of development (whether economic, social, or spiritual). More specifically he shows that as the need for relief (emergency response to disasters/calamities) receded and rehabilitation (refugee resettlement, reconstruction of housing, etc.) was completed, the MVS "transformative" experience began to lose both its meaning and motivation. Further, instead of unifying the European Mennonites, the diversity of interests and theology of the four groups hastened the demise of the MVS-MFD visionary program.

In terms of my earlier MCC experience in Korea and later as an MNN missionary in Japan, I have found troubling the North American Mennonite practice of a sharp differentiation between short-term relief and rehabilitation (MCC work) and the longer-term mission work/church planting (institutionalization/indigenization). Yet Redekop's volume illustrates the fact that ignoring differentiation can lead to "transmogrification." Indeed, this book needs to be read and pondered.

—*Robert Lee, Harrisonburg, Virginia, served in Europe and Korea under Mennonite Central Committee and in Japan under Mennonite Board of Missions and Mennonite Mission Network.*

AUTHOR'S PREFACE

This summer more than 300 young people joined together in 18 MVS camps in Western Europe. These young people not only said they were interested in their neighbor but wanted to prove their concern while learning to know him better. They expressed their convictions positively through constructing buildings such as houses for refugees, churches, children's homes and kindergartens, while at the same time bridging abysses of fear and mistrust which had existed.

Thus begins the first paragraph of the *MVS Newsletter*, November 1960 editorial, written by LaMar Reichert, MVS director in 1959-60. Reichert expresses rather clearly and concisely the major outlines of a significant youth movement that begin in posts World War II in Europe, which subsequently expanded worldwide.

The emergence of Mennonite Voluntary Service (MVS) in Europe is ironically based on a service idea that originated in Europe in the 1920s, spearheaded by the Swiss socialist Pierre Ceresole. His vision languished for some decades, largely because of the chaotic socio-political turmoil that was spreading over Europe, especially Germany, which culminated in World War II.[2] Fortunately, however, the voluntary service and work camps movement continued to be sporadically promoted by European peace groups in the 1920s and 1930s. The Quakers were especially active in European relief, which resulted in the formation of the American Friends Service Committee in 1917. [3]

Through this connection, the idea of voluntary service was imported and expanded in North America by the three Historic Peace Churches, [4] although other denominations also began to experiment with the idea. Then again ironically, the voluntary service idea and vision from the HPC perspective was reintroduced into Europe immediately following World War II. This intriguing development will become evident as the Mennonite Voluntary Service (MVS) story unfolds in the following pages. [5]

The magnitude and contribution of voluntary service today around the world is simply astounding. When the words *voluntary service* are Googled, the number of organizations, the types of programs, and the areas of the world in which they operate must be seen to be believed. [6] A scholarly article entitled "International Voluntary Service: Diplomacy, Development, Aid, or Self-Service?" reviews some of the leading literature on voluntary service. They conclude "international (voluntary) service has incredible potential as a social and economic development strategy." They also say that "More descriptive work is needed to assess exactly what these programs do and how they do it." [7]

This brief book focuses on a narrow slice of the worldwide voluntary service movement which has a unique and brief history. It reviews the history of Mennonite Voluntary Service in Europe and analyzes the reasons for its short life. The substance of the story will also heighten and then explain the "intriguing mystery" surrounding its rather sudden demise, or rather the transmogrification of MVS into other forms through which voluntary service continued to thrive in Europe and spread around the whole world. The European MVS story will also contribute to the understandings of the vision, nature, structure, and functions of voluntary service activities of the larger voluntary service movement, but of course from a unique faith perspective.

This is also a personal story. In January 1950, MCC sent me to Europe as a voluntary service worker for two years without a defined job or work. I had no idea what I was in for but trusted MCC and anticipated some excitement. I arrived in Rotterdam, the Netherlands, on the Veendam on January 17. After I passed through customs, an MCC worker loaded my baggage in the new Chevrolet van and drove through the city toward MCC headquarters.

Parts of Rotterdam were a surreal moonscape. Only the main streets had been cleared for traffic. The cityscape was unbelievable; there was hardly a building standing in the city near the port, and those that remained were heavily damaged. All the preparations I had received at MCC headquarters in Akron, Pennsylvania, did not prepare me fully for the emotional shock.[8]

I participated in the beginning of the MVS movement starting in March 1950 until December 1952 but have remained in touch with MVS through the years. I left the organization with considerable nostalgia and anxiousness, totally enamored of the excitement and significance of the work. Among the many highly rewarding personal consequences of the MVS experience was the opportunity to relate and to fellowship with so many people of all ages and stations, many of whom became my dear friends.

And traveling in Europe in subsequent years has been almost a hallowed experience, for I could revisit friends I had learned to know almost in every corner of Europe. I am still in touch with many, although the number is decreasing due to the limits of mortality. In addition, being exposed to and immersed in the magnificent culture of Europe changed my worldview indelibly. I can still vividly remember hearing for the first time Bach's "Cantata and Fugue in Dm" in the Frankfurter Dom, soon after my arrival.

My attempt to come to grips with the termination of MVS has helped me to understand how history evolves. It can be expressed through the injunction of the writer of Hebrews: "For here we have no permanent home, but we are seekers after the city which is to come" (Heb. 13:14). Seeking the permanency of human efforts is futile. But seeking the city which is to come is based on beginning to implement on earth the eternal goals and the eternal means needed to achieve them.

I have tried to present as accurate a picture as possible, though I was deeply involved in the story only at the beginning. It would of course be better if someone more detached and unbiased could write it. And it is my hope that someone will take up the challenge. But there is a need for deeper analysis, for if no one accepts the challenge soon, much of the personal experience will be lost and the movement may well be forgotten.[9] So this is my contribution to keeping that memory alive.

I have been helped in making it by many, including Hans-Joachim Wienss, for much invaluable information; Bob Lee for counsel; Loyal Klassen; for the fine photographs. My heartfelt thanks go to them as well as to Verna Goering, Milton Harder, Loyal Klassen, Bob Lee, LaMar Reichert, Ray Kauffman, and Howard Birky for publication subsidies.

—*Calvin W. Redekop*
Harrisonburg, Virginia

Hamburg, Germany, MVS work camp, 1948. Courtesy Milton Harder

European
Mennonite
Voluntary
Service,
1948-1972

Above: Ruins of Frankfurt central city.

Below: MVS office in MCC building, Frankfurt/Main, Germany

Chapter 1

THE FORERUNNERS OF MENNONITE VOLUNTARY SERVICE WORK IN EUROPE

A. The Early Sources of Voluntary Service

The European Mennonite Voluntary Service program described in this book has a rather convoluted and interesting history. As indicated in the Foreword, the original vision and idea of a voluntary service youth camp originated with Pierre Ceresole in Switzerland, one of the oldest republics in the world, with a standing army throughout most of its long history. He was born in 1879 of a Swiss army colonel father and lost his mother at age nine. He earned a Ph.D in Zurich in engineering and subsequently traveled and lived in United States (1909-1912) and Japan (1912-14). Ceresole returned to Switzerland in 1914. He wrote to the federal government, "I believe that the teachings of Christ are superior to the advices of the realistic politics and the commercial common sense . . . " and declared himself a pacifist.

Ceresole became familiar with the "peace movement." Traveling without a passport, he met in 1920 some German, Austrian, and English pacifists, including the Quaker Hubert Parris, and helped organize the Esnes work camp, near Verdun,

France, "the first camp of voluntary non-military national service." In 1924 Ceresole established in Zurich the "Swiss Action for the Peace" and became its first secretary. Then in rapid succession, he organized work camps in Lichtenstein (1928), France (1930), and Wales (1931), before ending with reconstruction in seven villages in India between 1934-1937. Ceresole incessantly confronted the Swiss state, assisted peace organizations, organized and led protests, was imprisoned, released, imprisoned, until he died on October 23, 1945, due to lack of exercise, poor food in prison, and resulting poor health. From 1937 through 1945 he thus became a "prisoner of the Eternal."[10]

The political turmoil of the 1920s and 1930s in Europe in which Ceresole worked was bound to stifle the vision of a peaceful world and that of enlisting idealistic young people in "building peace." So the European voluntary service movement became fragmented and moribund and was practically disbanded during World War II. Some work camps undoubtedly took place, but the movement and its ideals took a hiatus. It took the World War II catastrophe to revive this movement, and one of its expressions was Mennonite Voluntary Service.

B. American Voluntary Service Activities[11]

Meanwhile at the beginning of World War II, the Historic Peace Churches in America, namely the Church of the Brethren, the Mennonites, and Quakers, were busy with their own responses and alternatives to participation in the war. They focused especially on conscientious objection for draft-age young men. The Civilian Public Service (CPS) program was born as a consequence, beginning in May 1941. CPS was a hastily constructed program, massive in scale, and provided alternative service to war for 4,665 Mennonite and Brethren in Christ men along with many more from other denominations.[12]

CPS was basically successful, but among the most glaring problems was the feeling that the work was not important: Melvin Gingerich, author of the massive *Service for Peace* story of CPS states that "Working without pay and sometimes on jobs that appeared insignificant had a demoralizing effect on many men."[13] John D. Unruh, describing the variety of objections to the CPS program, notes that "there were of course, some who merely marked time and decided to 'sit it out.'" He observes that "They saw nothing in the program but the next week end or furlough, or better still final discharge. Some became cynical and somewhat resentful that the church had undertaken the administration of the program at all."[14]

The men discovered there were areas of national life tragically neglected by the CPS program, such as mental health and poverty pockets in inner cities.[15] These concerns were carried into the local congregations by the CPS men as well as the administration. Concluding his review of the CPS program, Unruh predicted that "being thrown into this common school of experience would translate into constructive and positive in the community and the church."[16] And he was right. Largely out of this experience Mennonite voluntary service was born.

Significantly, one of the neglected factors in the emergence of the voluntary service idea was the role women played in initiating the voluntary service idea. By 1945, women and wives of "drafted" conscientious objectors strongly promoted, almost demanded, being allowed to do their share in serving in an alternative way to military service. By late 1945 a group of CPS men presented a report which read in part, "There has been considerable agitation on the part of college women for some outlet in the form of service which would be comparable to that which the CPS boys are now giving in the mental hospitals."[17]

In September 14, 1946, the " MCC Executive Committee conditionally approved a limited number of supplemental voluntary service workers [in selected cities]."[18] The service projects soon expanded into various types of work, number of volunteers, and number of units. Elmer Ediger, MCC voluntary service director, described the growth:

> During 1950 the total Mennonite Voluntary Service program, aside from the regular relief program, included at least 125 one year volunteers and 800 short-term summer and winter volunteers. If we were to visualize this in an institutional figure, it would be the equivalent of a college student body of more than 300 for a nine month terms.[19]

The expanding and accelerating program is reflected in Ediger's listing of projects in which VSers were serving: "orphanages, delinquent homes, prisons, mental hospitals, in mission work in the cities, mountains, and rural areas . . . among Europeans, the Mexican and the Paraguayan people . . . and in various other types of teams." Thus Robert Krieder reported that "Seventy-eight young women served in the 1945 Women's Summer Service Program of MCC. This was the second year of the program, in 1944 there having been two units with 61 girls. The great majority of the girls favor continuation of this type of service in the future."[20]

C. The Voluntary Service
Idea Reimported to Europe

Ironically, the European voluntary service program that was to emerge was inspired in part by this fledgling American voluntary service program. The program had begun to take shape in 1944 in the United States and Canada and by 1950 was thriving.

In the meantime, as World War II was coming to an end, American Mennonites had already turned their attention to the European crisis and its implication for the fraternal Mennonite community of faith. After all, the Mennonite church in North America owed its very existence and its unique world view to its European ancestry, and there had been increasing interaction since the 1920s before World War II.[21]

Hitler's incomprehensible and unimaginably retrograde Nazi regime left the European people wounded, traumatized, defeated, and demoralized. The physical, mental, and spiritual destruction hung like a dark cloud over the continent when peace was declared in 1945. The victims of this destruction thus were receptive to any indication of hope and idealism to fill the vacuum Hitler's regime left behind.[22] Europe, but especially Germany, faced the massive clearing away of all the destroyed buildings, the rebuilding of the transportation system, the challenges of rebuilding the economic structures, and most of all, restoring functioning social institutions and healing broken national spirits.

Some early aspects of the volunteering motif were already applied in Europe in 1944, when MCC sent ten workers to London to prepare to work in Europe as soon as the door opened. MCC work in Europe, focusing mainly on relief, began in France in 1945 and continued through 1947. It consisted mainly of emergency food and clothing at first but expanded into refugee resettlement in Germany and abroad as the immediate needs receded. "Reconstruction and transport units" were already operating in Europe by 1946. "The first of these units was opened in Holland on the Island of Walcheren in the early spring of 1946. The island had been flooded by the Allied troops and was also the object of excessively [sic!] heavy bombing and shelling."[23]

A unit was sent to France in summer 1947 to reconstruct some farm homes for Mennonite families. "These units were integrated with the relief programs of emergency aid and often helped in food and clothing distributions. However their primary services were devoted to the reconstruction of buildings."[24] The units in France and Holland were administered by MCC while the unit in Belgium was directed by Mennonite Relief Committee (MRC.).

These construction projects were composed of males only, but in many other respects they were organic precursors to the work camps that were soon to follow. Irvin Horst describes the nature of unit members relationship to the local persons in charge of the reconstruction work, the families whose houses were being repaired and the local citizens, especially the young people. "Many friendly visits and meetings took place in the Quonset huts near Zoutelande, and in turn many unit members attended worship services, taught Sunday-school classes, and took part in youth activities of the Mennonite congregations."[25] About thirty-seven men worked in the three units, over a period of two years, all returned to regular MCC assignments or returned to the US after the camps were closed.

D. The Role of the
American Mennonite Colleges

A parallel activity contributing to the development of a voluntary service program was beginning to emerge as a result of the educational programs of the Council of Mennonite and Affiliated Colleges (CMAC). MCC relief workers in Europe had been brought into contact with many European Mennonite youth and felt they would benefit from an experience of living in American Mennonite communities. Thus in 1946 the CMAC started a Foreign Exchange Program. "The various Mennonite and Brethren in Christ colleges opened their doors in fall that year to Mennonite young people from Europe for a year's study"[26]—and in the first "five years brought 119 young people from Europe for a year of study in the Mennonite Colleges of America."[27]

This interaction increased the interest of American students for more contacts with European young people. Thus in 1947, the CMAC agreed to sponsor more with European youth. So a "group of young people from the American Mennonite colleges toured Western Europe and listened to lectures arranged for them at universities in Holland and Switzerland."[28] The students responded very positively, and it was decided to expand the program.

But the students had a strong feeling that there should be more direct and personal interrelationship and interaction between European youth and the American students. Hence the CMAC decided that "One of the most feasible means of bringing this to pass was through the avenue of short-term reconstruction and repair projects in devastated Germany."[29] Thus in the following year (1948) through the cooperative efforts of the CMAC; voluntary service administrators; MCC personnel; European Mennonites; military governments of the American, British and French zones; and local authorities, two units were set up in which American students could work one on one with European peers.

"Over one hundred Mennonite and Evangelical youth from various countries will participate in two voluntary service work camps this summer. They will run from July 9 to August 6, 1948."[30] The Ronneburg project involved renovating an old castle so it could be more readily used for youth conferences and religious groups. The other project was located in Hamburg and consisted of rebuilding a damaged assembly hall and erecting two barracks of a damaged epileptic and mental hospital operated by the Evangelische Kirche Deutschland (EKD).

These were truly international work camps with participants from the United States and Canada, the Netherlands, England, and Germany, totally new in Mennonite experience. The structure and activities of these two camps were typical of work camps generally: six hours of labor on the project, three meals and rest times, recreation, and educational activities including invited speakers and tours in the immediate area. MCC covered all the costs of the camps for the volunteers.[31]

An expansion of the summer projects took the form of smaller three week camps. The first one took place at Leutesdorf, "where a group of American and German Mennonite Youths helped to renovate an old building to be used as an old people's home." The second was conducted at Sembach, in the Pfalz, where the group composed of six American and nine Germans helped in the construction of a youth center for the South German Mennonites.[32] Another important project in the development of the MVS program, and subsequently Pax, was the Espelkamp program in North Germany, in the province of Westfalen in December begun in 1948.[33]

Espelkamp VS, German volunteers, 1949. Courtesy Milton Harder

Milton Harder, who had attended one of the work camps in 1948, was so challenged by MCC work that he opted to remain in Germany and served in MCC work camps in 1949 and then was given responsibility for overseeing the development of a newly emerging "long-term" voluntary service camp program at Espelkamp.[34] The specific project was to help the Evangelisches Hilfswerk (the relief arm of the EKD) in converting a series poison gas storage bunkers, which had not been discovered by the Allies, into houses for refugees from West Prussia, especially from the Danzig area.[35]

The camp opened in August 1948; in December MCC sent five boys to help Harder establish the camp. "The boys found almost unlimited possibilities for service both materially and spiritually."[36] "The boys went out each day to help the refugees build. There were tree stubs to dig out, old bricks to clean, walls to re-build, windows to put in, floors to lay, and many other tasks connected with building the refugee homes."[37] The volunteers soon found very concrete outlets for their presence, besides the physically demanding work. Boys and girls clubs, athletic games and other activities occupied the volunteers on week ends.

The European study-work summer program in 1949 was expanded to four projects, again with enthusiastic support from campers and receiving communities. At Hanover the camp built a barracks to house delinquent boys. The campers built a community recreational center in Stuttgart and began a home for delinquent girls in Frankfurt. The Krefeld camp in the lower Rhine area of West Germany focused on erecting "a prefabricated barrack to serve as a church and youth center in a refugee suburb called Osterath."[38]

Hanover, Germany, MVS work camp, 1949. Courtesy Milton Harder

None of the camp sites were luxurious; most of the campers lived in tents, cooked their own meals, and ate around camp fires. These conditions contributed to the comaradery and excitement of the camps.[39] Another project at Leutesdorf, referred to above, on the Rhine in fall 1949, was a "continuing camp" composed of twenty volunteers (including five on loan from Espelkamp). The volunteers worked to help "prepare the New Mennonite old people's home for occupancy."[40] (See Table 1, "Tabulation of International Work Camps," for details.)

E. The Influx of European Volunteers

It has been said that "nature abhors a vacuum." Beginning in 1939 and ending in 1945, World War II had been disastrous for Europe, especially for Germany, marked a drastic self-reevaluation of European history and culture, and was a turning point in Western history.[41] Especially among young people, the camps seemed a natural response to World War II impacts. Soon there was an influx of German, Dutch, and other volunteers who joined the Espelkamp program, mostly those who had already served in an earlier MCC work camp described above. Soon others volunteered to work in the program as they heard about it from their friends. Harder reported that

> By the end of two years (1948-1950) of camp operation, ninety-five young people had helped in Espelkamp's work camp. Of these, twenty-seven were American, sixty were Germans, four came from Holland, two from France, and one each from England and Switzerland.[42]

The Espelkamp project, in operation yet today, has a long distinguished history.[43] In many ways it was the "mother camp" of volunteering efforts in Europe. It also served as a temporary supply station for MCC volunteers awaiting assignments and as a training ground for camp volunteers who were then assigned to other VS locations, sometimes as leaders.[44]

Espelkamp, in north Westphalen, was consistently cloudy, windy, snowy, dreary and cold during the winter months. But despite this, volunteers came.[45] Further on the positive side, Espelkamp was becoming a home for refugee settlement and served as the model and inspiration for the summer camp program and for the other variations which subsequently emerged. It was the Espelkamp VS camp which had helped the Evangelischses Hilfswerk to contemplate and undertake the first resettlement program.[46] A byproduct of the project was the establishment of several congregations.[47]

Paul Peachey, at 1950 MVS reunion at Ruedesheim, Germany.

Westhofen, Germany, MVS work camp, 1950.

MVS Directors, Frankfurt, 1951. From left: Adriaan Swartendijk, Netherlands; Paul Peachey, MCC; Richard Hertzler, Germany; Ernest Hege, France; Cal Redekop; H. A. Fast, MCC Europe; Sam Gerber, Switzerland.

Chapter 2

THE CONTINUED DEVELOPMENT OF EUROPEAN VOLUNTARY SERVICE

The 1949 annual MCC meetings reported that the reconstruction of Europe was accelerating: "It is now felt that probably half of our personnel and budget will be used within Germany itself. The present winter may be the last one, where the major attention in Germany will be focused on mass emergency feeding and material aid distributions."[48] This situation was evident in the declining importance of emergency relief work in Europe generally, although food and clothing distributions continued in Germany. Other needs and opportunities for long-term needs were beginning to become more urgent.

In the meantime the work camps in 1948 and 1949 had created great enthusiasm and support among young people, especially in Germany. The awareness and conviction were emerging that these camps were important in serving the more long range social issues such as housing, recreation, international education, and the like. This change in focus of the European MCC program thus produced considerable personnel changes. Boyd Nelson, who had served in Italy as a relief worker, was brought to MCC headquarters at Basel and in early 1948 appointed director of European Voluntary Service.

But Nelson returned to America in December 1948 for personal reasons so Paul Peachey was appointed German "special projects" director for MCC, which included voluntary service. A war-damaged German home at Frankfurt/Main which had just been rehabilitated was leased in 1949 and became the new MCC center and also headquarters for the emerging voluntary service program.[49] His commission was to establish and strengthen the relationships between the Mennonite conferences, its leaders, and the young people with MCC's program.

MCC-sponsored international work camps in Europe from 1947 to 1950 had been planned and implemented with little participation on the part of the European Mennonites church leaders. But as the enthusiastic response of the Mennonite youth emerged continued to grow, the relationship between the American MCC workers and the European youth, especially the German, increased dramatically. This was augmented by the European youth who had been in North America in the educational exchange program administered by the CMAC. In addition the occasional "youth retreats" co-sponsored by MCC personnel and European youth leaders and the first "campers reunions" increased the relationship. Thus

> on September 23-26 (1948), a Campers Reunion was held at Ronneburg, the site of last year's student camps. About 75 attended, including MCC personnel, and a very strong interest and spirit prevailing. One camper wrote afterwards, "Believe me, you can look back on good success, most of us went out from those old walls with the feeling that actually and evidently God's blessing rested on the meeting."[50]

MCC provided transportation and food for these weekend retreats which guaranteed large attendance. The demoralization of the war, and the resulting lack of social programs and activities, much less work or employment, left a massive number of young people with little direction and hope, especially morally and spiritually. Thus one Dutch volunteer stated, "The camp meant for me a deepening of the reality that the Christian faith can bridge all sorts of gulfs and the expansion of spiritual insights and experience."[51]

If the enthusiasm expressed by ex-work campers is any gauge, the post World War II work camp movement filled the vacuum in a remarkable way.[52] Hans-Joachim Wienss, an early camper and later MVS director, states,

> My contact with MCC personnel in Enkenbach, in the Mennonitenhaus at Kaiserslautern, and later on in MVS camps, surely had an impact on young peoples' mind; it [it was] true for me in particular as well as in general. I could name several of whom I know this was the case.[53]

These camps and the reunions helped satisfy the hunger of the European youth for contacts among themselves and with Americans. The camps also provided a ready-made opportunity to be involved in some positive and constructive work in a setting that had been largely physically destroyed and culturally and socially demoralized. The personal relationships between MCC workers and the European youth was of great help in communicating the beliefs, ideals, and motivations of the American personnel, especially the gospel of peace and nonresistance, and convinced the European Mennonites of the sincerity of the Americans.[54] It was clear that the European Mennonite youth were infecting their congregations with the stories of exciting experiences and projects.

Thus by 1950, when MCC international voluntary service office in Frankfurt announced its summer program, a flood of applications arrived; in addition communities who had heard about the camps wrote letters appealing for help in needy projects resulting from the devastation of the Allied bombings. In addition, when the information about the camp program became more widely known in the Mennonite congregations, the response from the Mennonite youth also increased.[55]

By the time the 1950 summer work camp projects were made final, the openings were completely filled; each camp included European Mennonite youth, with Holland and Germany leading in the numbers of participation. The six camps ranged from a restoration of a home for the blind at Mulhouse, France, to participating in a work camp near Turin, Italy, at the Waldensian youth center called *Agape*, to Kiel, Germany, in constructing a barrack church for refugees.[56]

As VS director, it was my responsibility to search for potential camp sites, visit the site, discuss the project with the local responsible people, weigh pros and cons, evaluate their significance, and then make the decision to accept or reject the proposed project.[57] An example was the trip Paul Peachey and I took to investigate the Waldensian community near Turin in the high Italian Alps to check out the project noted above and the logistic arrangements. The scenery was even more breathtaking than the tourist posters and may have influenced our decision to accept the project.[58]

After selection of a site, more trips were often necessary to make sure all the complex and detailed arrangements with the community leaders were adequate and understood.[59] Thus I was introduced to postwar Europe, but especially Germany, in a manner that I realized only later was highly privileged. The geographic variety and beauty, the social and cultural histories and differences became my everyday fare.

Under the counsel and guidance of Paul Peachey, German MCC special projects director, and the European MCC director, I was privileged to travel through the beautiful countryside, which was less disturbed, in a little MCC Ford Taunus. These project evaluations provided close contact with innumerable "local denizens," such as village mayors and other city officials or church workers, and allowed taking nourishment at the ubiquitous *Imbisses* (food stands) and restaurants.[60] An almost daily event involved asking for road directions. Quicky I learned that the nearly universal German response, "*immer gerade aus*" (keep on straight ahead) was mostly the standard way of getting rid of undesired interruptions by these "foreigners."

By the end of summer 1950, the need for more leadership training in the summer camps and for a continuing voluntary service unit to provide service opportunities became very pressing. This was strongly expressed at a post-camp leadership conference held at Thomashof, near Karlsruhe, on August 28, 1950. It was also announced that though only four camps had originally been planned, by the time camp time had come, six camps had been arranged due to the pressure of eager participants.[61] Also the requests for the help and services MCC could offer came from a variety of petitioners, including MCC itself, and continued to grow. The idea of a mobile continuing work camp brigade (Caravan), able to respond to a variety of needs, was beginning to form.

Thus after the completion of 1950 summer work camps, it became clear that the MVS director could not be directing a growing movement without having a firsthand experience in a camp myself. So latter June and much of July at the Mainz Camp I spent at the Mainz project as co-leader with Walter Eisenbeis, a German war refugee:

> It had been my conviction that before I could adequately administer the VS program, I should experience what I was administering. So [it was decided] that I be co-director of the Mainz camp with Walter Eisenbeis. I chose the Mainz camp because it is close to the [MVS] office. Of course the danger existed that I [would] spend too much time in the office and not enough at camp. The 25th. was the day for start of the camp. I came a day late but got started despite that. It was a joy to be able to do physical work again after a pause of several years. The fellowship in the camp with the [variety of] people was very stimulating.[62]

Living intimately with twenty-five European young people at the Mainz camp provided many insights regarding the state of post-World War II conditions. One anecdote must suffice: One of the motivations to come to camp was to receive free lodging and food and broader experiences. MVS provided the meals, which consisted of fresh vegetables and other foods donated by local farmers, community churches, and other institutions; and MCC supplies, including canned meat, vegetables, and lard. Because butter was very expensive the camps often substituted MCC relief cans of lard for butter.

During the first supper after singing a German table blessing, as the lard was served, I noted that numerous volunteers took literally spoons full of lard and liberally ate it by the spoonful without spreading it on bread. I was rather irked and ready to announce that "the lard is a substitute for spreading on bread." My co-leader Walter Eisenbeis, a German refugee himself, quickly intervened: "You don"t know how hungry German people are for animal fats. This is a chance for them to recover a major hunger for animal fat." One major highlight, even a sensation, was the presence of two girls from the East Zone of Germany who had sneaked over the frontier to our camp.[63]

As indicated above, identification of projects, negotiating the various arrangements for lodging, free time activities, identification of what work the campers could do, the dangers involved, the need for supervision, health and accident contingencies, and many other elements required interminable communications, correspondence, and visits to the sites. But my experience at Mainz work camp confirmed the importance of the goal of all the work—namely the encounters of persons from such diverse backgrounds, experience, and culture which produced amazing realizations of the kinship of all peoples despite the differences in experience and outlook, and the reconciliation that could result from camp life.

The stream of refugees from the East increased, and the pressure to find housing and jobs and stability for the refugees by communities all over Germany mushroomed. Demand for volunteers to serve in a variety of need projects proliferated everywhere. Not only was the need great, but the desire for young people for service at varies times throughout the year, more specifically because often they were unemployed or had a vacation from regular work or free time. In September 1950 the idea was conveyed to MCC area directors for their information:

> You probably have heard of the proposed continuing international Mennonite work camp. The length of the participant's term would be immaterial although it would be well if they could spend at least three weeks. It is the beginning of a movement which we hope will make all [Mennonites in Europe] aware of the refugee problem as well as doing some practical work toward [solving] it.[64]

This was the germ of the idea which evolved into the International MVS Caravan, which is further described below. The high level of enthusiasm and solidarity in the camps again culminated in a "camper reunion" held on December 27-29, 1950, at Ruedesheim, in conjunction with MCC annual reunion. Sixty-five persons attended. Such MCC workers as C. F. Klassen and Benjamin Unruh, a leading Mennonite statesman, presented addresses at the reunion. MCC invited leading European Mennonite youth leaders, and several came, namely Samuel Gerber (the teacher), Ernest Hege, and Walter Mosiman. These were later founding members of the MFD (German for MVS).[65]

One example for a continuing year-around type of project which preceded the Caravan idea was already in process in September. By then preliminary plans had been made to begin a camp in the south Pfalz, at Offweilerhof near Zweibruecken, to help settle three Prussian Mennonite families on some land made available for refugee settlement. On October 16, the camp was officially opened.[66] Living conditions were primitive but very practical, since the team worked with the refugee families to initiate the construction of the farm home and other buildings.[67] The camp operated from October 1950 to January 1951 and had a total of ten participants, composed of German, Dutch, and American young people.[68]

One of the central realities of the work camp movement is the interpersonal bonding and affective relations that develop. This fact is so ubiquitous that it is taken for granted—it is so universal it is ignored. Several comments from an Offweiler camp report will illustrate.

Horst is a hard worker and is always prepared to make the best out of everything. We are grateful that he took time from his busy farm life to serve three weeks in the camp. Liesel is a hard worker and a good thresher woman for she can pitch bundles like a man. Her pancakes are always so tasty it is no wonder her brother eats so much. Mr. Loepp is a man who knows his history and has an interesting story to tell. He lost two of his sons in the war and later his wife, but to see his Christian courage is amazing. Svend loves to eat. There never was any trouble with any food left over when he was in our camp. Our great Dane was a strong man and his strength was a worthy contribution to our work project. Mel is an inspiration to our group and is always ready for a healthy laugh.[69]

*Above left: Gen. Lewis Her-
shey, U.S. Selective Service,
visiting Mainz, Germany, MVS work camp, 1951. Right: Milton Harder,
Kaiserslautern MCC office, Germany, 1951.* Courtesy Milton Harder

*Above: Digging
basement for
Student Center,
Mainz Univer-
sity, 1951.
Left: Dedication
of completed
Mainz Univer-
sity basement by
MVS, July
1951.*

Each MVS camp reflected the tantalizing mix of persons and characteristics from the various countries and cultures. These have remained in the memory of every camper.

With the arrival of additional volunteers from America, more flexibility was allowed in the work camp format and the formation of the "MVS Caravan." Four American MCC volunteers arrived in Germany in fall 1951, consisting of Hugo Friesen, Curt Janzen, Bob Lee, and Sol Yoder. The first project was at Haus der hilfenden Haende at Bienrode, New Braunschweig, where they provided friendship and support for German refugee boys. The work aspect involved tearing down an old building in preparation for a youth center.

The second project, which included Bim Noe, a Dutch volunteer, along with several Mennonite refugees opened a project at Zeilsheim (near Frankfurt) in January 2, 1952, which consisted of helping to work on a new church building to house a new refugee congregation including some Mennonites.[70] Several Pax fellows, Albert Roupp and Willard and Richard Rush, were also later sent there to continue in the construction helping the church move toward completion. Richard Rush wrote in his diary, "Later, Willard Rush and I were sent back to work with the German contractor, Herr Steinbach. We worked at Zeilsheim from April 3 until May 15. When we left the rafters were up but the building was far from finished."[71]

The "Caravan" idea flourished. After the Zeilsheim project, the Caravan moved to Backnang, from February 26 to May 17, 1952. Their project focused on preparing a deteriorating hotel for the soon arriving Pax unit. Four Dutch volunteers joined the unit.

> For the MVS Caravan, stop number three, Backnang, served the dual role of a continuing international work camp and of a liaison group for MCC (Pax) and the refugees. Because the Pax unit did not arrive until the middle of May, the Caravan had literally dug and laid the foundation for the future builder's group. Concurrently, with the incipience of the building project, numerous contacts and arrangements were made with the refugees and the contractors etc to develop a "going program." With its dual role here, the Caravan's dual

purpose of creating community interest and of fostering the spirituality of its own group, became even more important. The Caravan group worked on the project over 3,350 hours; a drainage system was built, three full basements dug, two house foundations poured to ground level and the outside walls of the first house built. With the arrival of the Pax group, the Caravan moved on, leaving a work clearly started. Since that time Pax, refugees and other VSers have completed four of the ten six-family homes.[72]

Caravan moving to Windishgarsten, Austria, MVS project, 1952. Courtesy Richard Rush

This mobile MVS work camp unit, dubbed the MVS Caravan, had been in the conceptually formative and development stages. By May 18, the Caravan had left for Windishgarsten, Austria, to help build a church building for some Protestant refugees from Romania, which had been begun by Brethren Service volunteers at a summer camp a year earlier. This reflected the evolution of a more formal status of the Caravan.

At the concluding farewell campfire (June 13, 1952), an elder of the small congregation related again the story of fifty years of unsuccessful efforts to build a Congregational meetinghouse and now spoke of joy in seeing the building become a reality. As he thanked the Caravan, one felt that God's hand was very definitely directing the building of this church; more than that, the presence of MVS in a measure had revived and strengthened these people in their faith in God and Christian brotherhood.[73] The MVS Caravan volunteers returned to their respective homes, but the long-term MCC personnel in the Caravan returned to Frankfurt, at which time they were assigned leadership positions for the 1952 summer work camps which were only several weeks away The *MVS Newsletter* reports,

> The Caravan has just returned from Austria where they worked on a church building in a refugee settlement area. After the summer camps (in which the Caravan members served) the Caravan will again work at various places. Probably the first place will be Leutesdorf, on the Rhein, where we will build a road to a Friedhof for an old peoples home.[74]

The MVS Caravan operated for several years as a mobile unit that would open long-term projects, other short term projects, and to provide experienced summer work camps leaders.[75]

The 1952 summer work camp schedule consisted of four camps, namely at Ruenthe, Hohenlimburg, Nuernburg, and Linz. They all took place between July 28 and August 30. The work at Ruenthe consisted of helping homeless miners in the Ruhr valley accumulate 2000 hours of self help to qualify for Government loans. Hohenlimburg. project was similar to the Ruenthe, but the recipients were recent refugees from all parts of Germany.

> The "Evangelische Baugemeinde" had been so impressed with the work and witness of the Pax Builders Unit in Espelkamp that they requested through MCC that a similar work camp to build a settlement in Hohenlimburg [be established].[76]

The post-World War II European young people's interest expanded so rapidly that the voluntary service work camp organizations began looking for orientations and consultation. In response the United Nations Educational and Scientific Organization (UNESCO) established a Coordination Committee For International Voluntary Work Camps (CCIVWC) in 1949 headquartered in Paris, France. The goals were to support and coordinate the work camp activities of the many groups that were operating volunteer service programs.[77] The stated purpose of this organization was "to provide a permanent office which would encourage information exchange between the many work camp organizations in Europe."[78]

The Autumn 1953 CCIVWC report lists Europe, America, Asia, and Africa as the continents in which some thirty-five countries had work camps conducted by a variety of organizations.[79] Mennonite Voluntary Service was listed among the seventeen organizations conducting camps in Europe. CCIVWC sponsored conferences on the issues, objectives, and problems of work camps and even provided funds for specific projects and conferences. MVS was a beneficiary of several grants. Later a number of Pax men were loaned to help with the coordination work in Paris, beginning in 1954 and including William Beitel, Paul Boyer, Paul Kissel, LaMar Reichert, Rodney Penner, and Orville Schmidt.[80] (See Table 2.)

Another organization was formed to help with coordinating the activities of the organizations serving in Europe whose major goal was promoting peace, namely the Association of International Work Camps for Peace (AIWCP). The AIWCP was an organization created to "give a special testimony to peace by organizing peace seminars and work camps with peace emphasis" and focused especially on Germany.[81]

A coordinating association called *Arbeitskreis Internationale Gemeinschaftsdienste* (AIG) was established in Germany which acted as conduit for considerable financial assistance from the German government, based on the recognition of the impressive service these work camps were providing for the many dislocated German youth, as well as the home construction it provided for German refugees.[82] For a number of years, the German Government assisted work camps financially. For example, in 1955, MVS director LaMarr Kopp presented a financial report to the AIG, which reported that the camps had cost 14,699 DMs (Deutsche Marks) and received a grant from the *Bundesjugendplan* (German Federal Youth Dept.) for 3,846 DMs.[83]

These social/economic conditions and the resulting organizations provided the historical and contemporary milieu in which the European Mennonite Voluntary Service program naturally emerged. The international work camp activity, especially in Europe, was obviously much larger than the Mennonite program, though MVS was not the smallest in the promotion and support of these developments.[84]

As the programs mushroomed, the recruitment of campers and the appointment and training of camp leaders became an additional obligation carried out by the director. From the beginning MCC had covered all of the director's expenses, since in the formative years an MCC worker was director. The MVS council proved helpful by offering the names of young people in their congregations who might be just right for participation in camps and also for becoming camp leaders. They also suggested projects in their own areas with which the council members were familiar. Thus for example a MVS Camp Leaders Conference was held at Frankfurt, on June 16, 1952, and the leaders and the summer camps for 1952 were introduced.

The MVS Caravan members were part of this conference since as indicated above they also provided some of the "reserve" leadership for the camps. Major topics for the day-long seminar included "Evangelism versus ecumenicity; getting democratic living principles across; [and] the Ideology—what can we give?"[85]

The work camps and the MVS Caravan activities developed many related consequences; among the most important were the lasting friendships and relationships among the volunteers, the leaders of the projects, MCC and MVS officers and administrators. As indicated above, already in the fall of 1950 a retreat of ex-campers was held in Leutesdorf, which attracted sixty-five participants from Denmark, France, Germany, Holland, Switzerland, Canada, and the U.S. The Mennonite conferences in the four sponsoring countries (France, Germany, Netherlands, and Switzerland) saw the significance of MVS for their youth and thus youth conferences were held to capitalize on the enthusiasm that MVS was creating.[86]

A Post Camp Leaders Conference became an annual event conducted after the summer work camps were completed. Participants included the leaders of the various camps, the MVS caravan leadership, the MVS board (when possible), and the MVS director and staff. The strengths and weaknesses of each camp were reviewed and noted. The 1954 conference for example examined, among other issues, whether there should be fewer projects if adequate prior investigation of all the contingencies could not be made in time; further there were concerns that the leaders should be Christian and Mennonite if at all possible; co-leaders should not be both the same sex—ideal was where "she oversees the kitchen and domestic aspects," (sic) and he oversees the project. Participants should be older, at least eighteen to thirty-five, rather than under sixteen, and persons should not see this as a "cheap vacation."[87]

The potential for MVS not only to respond to emergency needs of post-World War II Europe but also to be a means for recruiting and inspiring young people for more "normal" humanitarian and religious service soon became apparent to the MVS council. At the February 16, 1952, meeting of the MVS council held in Basel, the topics for discussion in preparation for the following year included: 1) MVS secretariat issues; 2) the program for 1952 summer camps, resettlement plans (MVS Caravan and the emerging Pax program; 3) youth work with MFD help, including Bible camps, youth meetings and retreats, and related activities, such as sponsoring an international youth meeting in conjunction with the Mennonite World Conference, which met from August 12-15, 1952); and 4) finances, including application to Bonn for subsidies, getting the four countries to contribute their fair share of the financial costs, and the purchase of a Jeep for various MVS needs.[88]

The report *Die Jugend auf der Weltkonferenz* (Youth at the World Conference), namely the Mennonite World Conference held in Zurich, Switzerland, in August 1952, provides a concise picture of the conditions of Mennonite youth in Europe at that point. A roster of youth leaders, including Hans Gerber (Switzerland), Hans Galle and Theo Glick (Germany), Jacques Graber (France), Jan de Vries (Holland), Peter Wiens (Paraguay), and Myron Ebersole (U.S.), presented descriptions of the spiritual status of the young people. The reports were remarkably similar, indicating that the youth were losing close ties to the church and were being "seduced or tempted " by the world, especially in sports and mass entertainment.

After the presentations on the "congregation and its youth" a "A Working Session on International Mennonite Voluntary Service" was held. Without exception the responses overwhelmingly supported the significance of the MVS program. A major part of the session dealt with concerns about the lack of support by Mennonite national conferences, the need to get more youth to see the value of voluntary service, and how the education of the voluntary service vision could be promoted. The European representatives strongly encouraged and thanked MCC for launching and supporting the program and implored MCC not to forsake the program "half finished."[89]

The next *Jugendleiter Seminar* (Youth Leaders seminar) was held at Leutesdorf, in December 1952. A broad range of topics was discussed, including the revitalization of the rite of baptism, better working together of pastors and the youth of the congregations, the need for instituting Sunday schools in the face of the neglect of Christian education in the homes. Among the conclusions this conference reached was the mandate to produce a Youth Work Information Newsletter which the MVS office, now located in Basel, was to direct, coordinate, and produce.[90]

As is discussed further in chapter four, I left the MVS work in December 1952. I had been involved in the development of both MVS and the emerging Pax program for three years. Since both programs were focused on the same objectives, namely providing service opportunities for the youth and serving European emergency needs, the early activities of both organizations were relatively similar and mutually complementary. However by December 1952 it was clear that the programs had grown so much that they were in need of separate leadership, so my resignation was an appropriate occasion for a change in leadership. Thus separate directors for MVS and Pax were appointed.[91]

Jan W. de Vries, a participant in several MVS camps, and then participating in helping develop the Caravan, became the second director of MVS in January 1953. In his first report as director, he describes the continuing work of the Caravan:

> On February 1, the flood catastrophe took place in Holland. I immediately went to Holland, and already on February 3, the Caravan was on its way from Guebweiler to Holland. I found a project directly in the needy area: e.g. in Wolphaartsdijk (island of Zuid-Beveland) were we went February 10. After having worked there

for some weeks—cleaning about 35 houses—the Caravan moved to Kortgene where they did the same work for one week.[92]

There were also the usual summer camps during the year, including two in Germany and two in Austria. De Vries reports that there were 124 participants. They came from France—11, Germany—30, Holland—40, Switzerland—4, Romania—1, and U.S.—30. The MVS work camp program was, however, also continuing the emergency work in Holland with two continuing camps.[93] This operation was the largest work ever undertaken by MVS and lasted the longest. Begun by the Caravan in February 1953, it continued for several years, including summer work camps. Pax fellows were sent to help organize and operate the camps, illustrated by Roger Hochstetler, who arrived in March 1953 and served in the Holland flood rehabilitation until he returned to the United States in 1954.

In spring 1954, LaMarr Kopp became director of MVS. Six MVS work camps were conducted during the summer, one in Kerkwerve, Holland, which consisted of demolishing houses damaged by the massive floods of 1953. Young people came from many countries to help with the rehabilitation including volunteers donated by International Voluntary Service (IVS). The Dutch Mennonite Church generously supported the projects with financial assistance and personnel.

The other camps were at Mainz, Elmshorn, Berlin-Heilegensee, Salzburg, Bod Godesburg, and in Greece. In September, LaMarr Kopp traveled to Algeria to "investigate the possibilities of opening an emergency work camp in the Orleansville region. Because of several important reasons it did not seem wise for MVS to move into that area with a camp immediately."[94]

It is instructive to look at the global picture regarding the work camp phenomenon. Table 2 cited earlier provides the information on a global scale for the year 1954, compiled by the Co-ordination Committee for International Voluntary Work Camps sponsored by the United Nations Educational and Scientific Organization (UNESCO), which was headquartered in Paris. However, the overwhelming majority of work camps were centered on the European continent, where the ravages of World War II were the greatest. MVS reflected this profile.

This table provides a fine overview of the variety of aspects of the global voluntary service activities. The objectives of the organizations, the projects they undertook, and the international distribution were extremely varied. A comparison over the years would be highly instructive in terms of where and when the needs emerged and how the voluntary service organizations responded. The comparative material remains to be compiled.[95]

The organizational structures of the camps also varied greatly. Unlike many other organizations, MVS because of its intentions of integrating the European Mennonites into the program experimented with a number of forms—weekend camps, week-long camps, and mobile camps, such as the MVS Caravan noted above, all of which were aimed at attracting European Mennonite youth and making it possible for them to participate. Thus for example the MVS Caravan was mobilized in an unusual project in October 1954, when D. C. Kauffman, European MCC director,

> made a trip to Greece to investigate the need for relief food and clothing in the earthquake areas of Thessaly. He saw much destruction and need and asked the American Mennonites to send food and clothing which could be distributed. MVS accepted the assignment of distributing this (sic) relief goods. On December 20, two English boys, Bill Roff and Paul Glanville, Dutch boy, Piet de Graff, and one American left Basel, Switzerland as the first MVS team to accept the assignment of relief distribution. Part of the time the MVS team lived with the American boys of the Pax Services, which has two units in Macedonia. The MVS team was joined in Greece by another English boy, Tom Braun from the FAU team on the Ionian Islands. The group finished the distribution about 1. April, 1955.[96]

MVS work in the 1954 Holland floods produced another interesting development. LaMarr Kopp reported to the MVS council:

> During my stay in Holland I also visited Mr. van Giles, an active worker in the Mennonite Peace Group. We dis-

cussed the CO problem in Holland and he told me that if MVS would find a worthy long-term project in Holland, he would take this project to the proper authorities and make a request that a group of Dutch CO's be allowed to work on this project. If this would materialize, a significant and history-making event would have occurred, inasmuch as the Dutch government has never even considered such a proposal before.[97]

The program expanded in 1955 to include five work camps at Bad Godesberg, Holland, Elmshorn, Vienna, and Berlin plus the work in Greece. Ongoing work in Holland took place in

> the small village of Nieuwerkerk, on Schouwen-Duiveland, badly hit by the floods of 1953. Practically the whole island was under water from February to October. After three attempts the last break of the dike, near Nieuwerkerk, was repaired, and then began the monumental tasks of cleaning up and bringing back to life Schouwen-Duiveland. Two work camps brought in volunteers to help in the cleaning up. Gradually some houses were made liveable, and new ones were built. Even this summer though, over 100 residents were still living in wooden barracks a couple of miles away.[98]

MVS was again considering a "continuing" work camp, and announced that

> MVS is planning to open a new continuing camp. We need volunteers for this project and we hope you and your friends will be able to spend some time with us. The work is construction of a playground for the community. The camp will open May 2 and continue through the summer.[99]

The camp at Vienna focused on the restoration of the old Protestant Karlschule, which had been launched by the Church of Brethren Service Commission and soon joined by the Mennonite Central Committee through its Pax program.[100] One of the campers reports on the experience:

> Picture, if you can 25-30 young men and women from eleven nations living and working in a war-gutted four-

story brick building in the heart of beautiful Vienna, that city of cities with its own very special atmosphere. . . . We had torn down brick walls, cleaned the brick, hauled out the rubble, leveled the floors, and cemented. As we left for home we could see our memorial, accomplished for the good of the school [and] bring the nations of the world together into a more complete understanding.[101]

The other camps at Bad Godesberg, Elmshorn, and Berlin dealt with renovation of a castle and refugee housing, respectively.[102] The MVS camps in 1956 and 1957 moved toward more diverse projects and sponsors such as those in Berlin. In 1956 a camp in the French sector of Berlin focused on helping the German Red Cross construct a kindergarten for all the refugee families that were streaming into Berlin. It seems the German Red Cross and other organizations were becoming aware of the contribution that MVS was making, especially in Germany.

Hence two projects were also conducted in Berlin in 1957. One was located right behind Tempelhof Airport, the scene of so many dramatic events. It was similar to the project in 956, but in a different part of Berlin. A second project in Berlin in 1957 consisted of renovating an old building to be used for some of the "4,000 persons per week from the Soviet occupied zone of German [who] continue to cross the border and flee to the West." One camper wrote, "A summer of service in this unusual metropolis, sometimes referred to as the 'Meeting Place of the World' where East and West meet in an atmosphere of tension and mistrust, is a never-to-be forgotten experience."[103]

A project at Hoernum/Sylt in north Germany (July 15-August 18) illustrates the broadening of MVS service. In this case the project was assisting a boys home, sponsored by five north German cities. The buildings which were

originally put up to provide vacation quarters for 40 officials of Hitler's army, now serve about 600 children. At this place MVS is planning to have a small group of volunteers working with the youngsters, playing with them, taking them on hikes, going swimming with them and arranging other recreational activities for them. Here is another opportunity to leave a silent testimony of service and concern. For those persons interested more in a social service project than in a construction unit, this camp should be particularly inviting.[104]

Another illustration of the broadening of the MVS perspective was the launching of a series of Easter Work camps. In 1956 two Easter camps were held at Bad Duerkheim and Burhave. Their success resulted in four camps lasting between five days and fifteen days in 1957. They were operated in Steenwijk, Netherlands; Zeist, Netherlands; Fontette, France; and London, England. Some of these camps were initiated and spearheaded by ex-MVS campers who had "caught the voluntary service 'spirit.'" Thus for example

> Two enthusiastic MVS'ers in England, Sally Aldworth and Maureen Harvey, are arranging on their own initiative, an interesting Easter MVS project. The group will paint and redecorate the kitchen and staircase of a community center in the East End of London.[105]

A combined MVS and Pax workcamp was conducted at Warga, Friesland, Netherlands, June 17-August 19, 1956. Some fifty volunteers served varying amounts of time at the camp, coming from eight countries—namely Austria, England, Germany, Lebanon, Norway, Switzerland, U.S., Sweden. The goal of the project was the construction of a small Doopsgezinde Church and started literally "from the ground up." It was practically completed when the group left. The rapport among the campers and with the community was remarkable, as evidenced by the numerous very favorable regional newspaper reports as well as the support from the people in the community including providing food such as freshly baked bread.[106]

The MVS Easter weekend work camps continued. They allowed many students and employed persons to attend. For example in 1959, there were two camps, one in Valkeveen, Holland, and one in Guebwiller, France. During summer 1959 ten international camps were conducted, located in France, Greece, Austria, Germany, West Berlin, and Holland. Further MVS reunions were held after the busy summer of camps.

Thus the October 31-November 2 reunion at Valkeveen, Holland, was reported in the *MVS Newsletter*.[107] In 1960 MVS sponsored the "second annual MVS reunion" in Germany. Fourteen camps were conducted in 1960, including one in Israel.[108]

The MVS program in Europe grew and flourished (see Table 1). It continued to attract an amazing sampling of international volunteers and religions, as indicated in Tables 2 and 3. And requests for assistance continued to arrive at the MVS office. In 1957, eighteen camps were conducted, (four Easter and fourteen summer) with little change until 1960. During these years there were Easter camps and summer camps, and camps were organized in Austria, Switzerland, France, Germany, West Berlin, Holland, England, and Spain. Church affiliation numbered twenty-nine different religious traditions, including an average of around forty persons whose religious affiliation was either "none" or "unknown." Many of the camps were repeat camps, as for example in Berlin, where between 1960 and 1962, five camps were conducted,

One MVS project deserves specific attention—the Witmarsum Mennonite Church project, also known as the Menno Simons Memorial Church. Located in the village of Witmarsum, birthplace of Menno Simons, the Netherlands, it was one of seventeen projects conducted by MVS during 1960. It was a sizable project, with two summer camps staged consecutively, namely early June through late August, and was built with the assistance of Pax men. The dedication of the building took place on January 22, 1961.[109]

Built near the Menno Simons monument, the church building serves as a historical "pilgrim shrine" in memory of Menno Simons, early Mennonite leader.[110] By 1961, MVS offered three thirteen-day "Easter Camps," at Salzburg, Austria; Liverpool, England; and Bad Duerkheim, Germany; three thirty-day "spring camps" at Grenoble, France; Neumarkt, Austria; Odessa, Greece; and Ardeche, France; and eight summer camps varying in length from four to six weeks in Sulz, Austria; Berlin, Germany; Graz, Austria; Surrey, England; Agadir, Morocco; Adreche, France; Ionnina, Greece; and Alt-Aussee, Austria (see Tables 1-3).

It is clear that the venues and projects were even more varied and extensive. The nature of projects included repairing or remodeling buildings, for youth centers and children's homes;

improving sanitation facilities; constructing playgrounds, religious centers, schools, water reservoirs; and laying water pipes.[111] MCC continued to underwrite the MVS (and Eirene) program by funding the MVS executive secretary position. From 1954 to 1956, LaMarr Kopp from Pennsylvania was director. During his tenure the cooperation of Pax and MVS expanded, illustrated by the extensive references to Pax men and their activities.[112]

Erwin Goering succeeded Kopp and served as director from 1956, when the office was moved to Kaiserslautern, to summer of 1959, when LaMar Reichert assumed the responsibility.[113] The desire to transfer the leadership to the European Mennonites was finally implemented in 1962, when Jaap Rem from the Netherlands was installed. The directors, nationalities, and terms below show the degree to which MCC directly financed MVS and the amount of turnover.

MVS Directors

Calvin Redekop, USA	1950-1952 (Dec.)
Jan de Vries, Netherlands	1953-1954 (April)
LaMarr Kopp, USA	1954 (May)-1956 (deceased)
Erwin C. Goering, USA	1956 to 1959 (deceased)
LaMar Reichert, USA	1959-1960
Jaap Rem Netherlands	1961 (May)-1962 (May)
Hanspeter Bergthold, Germany	1963 (April)-1965 (April)
Joerg Isert, Germany	1965(May)-1969 (Sept.)
Han-Joachim Wienss, Germany	1969 (Aug.)-1971 (June)[114]

Source: MVS Newsletters, MMC files, personal files and correspondence including Kopp and Wienss. Of course many people helped in the office and on the field. It is impossible to list all of them, but the following list illustrates the range: Lenie de Groot, MVS director in Holland, Loes Jansen Kramer, secretary, Holland; Jim Besse, Robert Steiner, Garth Hershberger, Howard Birky, Nelson Good, field assistants; and Piet de Graaf, Holland, who helped organize MVS camps in Holland. The MVS connections with UNESCO in Paris were managed by Paul Boyer, Glen Good, Rodney Penner, Allen Schmidt, and Orville Schmidt.

By 1959, MVS had expanded to ten work camps: Kaernten and Vienna, Austria; Sylt, West Berlin, and Salzgitter, Germany; Hinterbruehl, Austria; Guebweiler, France; Arnissa, Greece; Salzburg, Austria; Bussum, Holland. It is clear that the locations indicated a widening of the net of MVS locations for projects, though Germany still led with three projects. With the acceleration of volunteer programs and the increasing needs in all parts of the world, as well as increased peace activities by American Christian denominations, additional voluntary service actions were launched.

A total of 262 camps were operated from 1948 to 1971.[115] The high point was reached in 1962 with 20 camps. Germany received the most help with 96 camps, followed by France and Austria who tied with 35 each. The Netherlands benefitted from 24 camps, while Greece received help with 14 camps. Great Britain was the site of nine camps, Switzerland conducted seven camps, while Israel and Belgium had four camps each. Algeria, Morocco, Spain, Luxemburg, and Yugoslavia had one each.[116] Adequate statistics are not available regarding the actual number of volunteers that served in these camps, but if an conservative average of 18 volunteers per camp is used, a total of 4,338 volunteers served during this decade and a half.

The needs for service were increasing in all parts of the world; similarly the need for heightened "peace witness" by the "Historic Peace Churches" seemed apparent. And the opportunities for witnessing to the "way of peace" and the Christian faith itself was increasingly noted by the Mennonite MVS representatives, especially the French and the Swiss. Testimonials of the values of MVS fill the records of MVS. One randomly selected provides the bridge to the next section:

> At the MVS campers reunion at Heerewegen Holland we discussed with pleasure the work we had done and recounted the many expressions of thankfulness the beneficiaries expressed in the catastrophic conditions they found themselves in. But we also questioned how can we now in our everyday life, each at his own position, apply the experiences we have had at camp—the voluntary comradeship in the service of the love of neighbor? We had the happy conviction that voluntary service was a good way to help the neighbor. Thus we committed ourselves to tell many others of this way, because there is still great need for voluntary service. (Berndt Greafe, *MVS Newsletter*, Jan. 1954)

Council of Menonite and Affiliated Colleges students. Frankfurt, 1951

Chapter 3

THE EXPANSION/
DIVERSIFICATION OF
SERVICE

Based on stories camp participants brought back to local congregations, leaders of the European Mennonite conferences
began to believe that voluntary service was a chance to work on
the "mission field." The major elements in the MVS operations
from the 1949 to 1972 presented above give an overview of the
massive opportunities for relating (and witnessing) to others.

However it is necessary to place the MVS, its growth,
changes and termination into the context of MCC's mandate,
the European Mennonite community, the youth movement that
was regnant at the time, as well as the economic and social conditions in general to understand the differing "theological pre-
suppositions" of MCC and the European Mennonites. It is this
difference in orientation that will be explored more fully in
chapter 5 dealing with the demise of MVS.

The material, social, and spiritual vacuum that existed, especially in Europe, but also in other parts of the globe, had resulted in the proliferation of new voluntary service visions and
organizations in many parts of the world, as already alluded to
above. One example is International Voluntary Service (IVS),
with which MVS developed some rather productive relations.

> International Voluntary Services was founded in 1953
> by a combination of people with backgrounds in reli-

gion, government, agriculture and social services. Its primary purpose was to use the services of volunteers on an organized basis to combat hunger, poverty, disease, and illiteracy in the underdeveloped areas of the world, and thereby further the peace, happiness and prosperity of the people.[117]

Mennonite Central Committee, the Church of the Brethren, the Quakers, and other denominations were among participants and sponsors. A reason for the creation of IVS was the

> effort to extend limited denominational resources to areas of the underdeveloped world. Together they were able to develop programs in underdeveloped areas that were approved for alternative service and financed by the United States government.[118]

Thus a number of American Mennonite IWs, as well as conscientious objectors from the other peace churches, and other denominations such as Methodists had a ready-made organization and channel to serve in various places around the world. "During the war period of 1960-75, IVS sent most of its volunteers to Southeast Asia. At one point there were more than 200 IVSers serving in Vietnam [sic] and Laos."[119] From its beginnings, the IVS voluntary service program provided opportunities for many young people to serve in a variety of work in far flung locations without having to be limited to what the denominational organizations were doing.[120]

One early example of the Mennonite involvement was Carl Jantzen's assignment to IVS in Pakistan. Carl had served in Iraq, on loan from Pax, in 1953.[121] An even wider net for MVS was cast when appeals from European church leaders to respond to the humanitarian disasters in Morocco, which resulted in another new voluntary service organization:

> In February 1957, Dr. W. A. Visser 't Hooft, general secretary of the World Council of Churches, challenged the Historic Peace Churches to open a program of peace and service in North Africa—an area of abject economic deprivation. The idea, encouraged by Heinz Kloppenburg, German Oberkirchenrat, and Andre Trocmé—a French Reformed pastor and secretary of the International Fellowship of Reconcilia-

tion—was accepted "in principle by the Brethren and Mennonites."[122] This caused the MVS and the Brethren Service Commission offices to investigate more closely the situation there. The response was immediate. "The entire project, beginning with the idea and challenge, took less than a year to implement. On August 12, at Karlsruhe, Germany, the name *Eirene* (International Christian Service for Peace) was adopted for the project." [123] The Brethren Service Commission, Mennonite Central Committee, and International Fellowship of Reconciliation (IFOR) became charter members. Other sponsors were invited, "providing they were willing to embrace the purposes and ideals of Eirene, and were prepared to make the necessary financial commitments."[124]

The purpose of Eirene was to provide

voluntary and Christian service in lands suffering from political, social, and economic tensions and in areas of emergency and distress and in this way contribute toward understanding between peoples and toward world peace.[125]

The *Handbook* given to all volunteers clearly stated that "participants must show evidence of a personal commitment to Jesus Christ as Savior and Lord of their life."[126] Kreider comments that the "sponsoring agencies firmly believed that war and violence were contrary to the life and teachings of Christ." MVS became the European MCC representation in the program. A number of MVS and Pax fellows served in the Morocco Eirene work.

Quakers and other agencies also sent volunteers.[127] The original group was composed of five men, two French, two Dutch, and one American. The first program in Morocco flourished and developed into a wide variety of activities, including experimental farming and agricultural development, community education on health care and literacy, training in the construction of animal shelters and later homes, assisting in refugee resettlement resulting from the disastrous earthquakes, and intervening in tribal conflicts.[128]

Eirene expanded from Morocco to Europe at the invitation of the German Evangelical Church (EKD), which sponsored numerous projects including hospitals and educational institutions. In 1961 the German government recognized Eirene as an alternative service to war program but did not allow foreign service placement.[129] MVS, which had processed the volunteers for the Eirene, became the official representative for Germany when the Eirene operations were divided between the respective countries: "Since April 19, 1966 Eirene has a German [Mennonite] structure, which operates independently, similar to the Swiss, who are operating an independent program as well."[130]

Kreider states that by the end of the 1960s, Eirene's official relation to the German ecclesiastical realm became problematic so it was decided that "the German Church accept responsibility for managing and financing Eirene." But this is directly challenged by Hans Joachim Wienss, who states that "Eirene has always been organically linked to its founders, which includes MCC and the BSC and IFOR. Eirene is still an independent body sponsored by the above mentioned organizations."[131]

This program then provided the channel by which German conscientious objectors could serve in state approved projects.[132] The Eirene program was expanded to serve projects in Cyprus, Congo, Nigeria, and Rhodesia (sic). The German government fully recognized the Eirene program as a place for German COs could serve and it has continued in that role.

A brief excursus into the Pax phenomenon is also necessary at this point, for as already indicated very early the MVS program and the Pax program developed along parallel lines and interacted in very meaningful ways. In fact, it can be said that the germs of the Pax program were inherent in the MVS vision. As implied above, by 1950 the MVS camp program had become very well entrenched and effective in providing a meaningful experience for the campers plus addressing material needs such as cleanup of war destruction, reconstruction of damaged structures, and community rehabilitation.

The increasing possibility of war with North Korea resulted in the United States' Congress' passage of the "Universal Military Training and Service Act" on June 19, 1950. This energized the MVS leaders, because they speculated that with the established voluntary service program in Europe, the possibility of having American I-W fellows serve in Europe seemed an achievable goal. This was especially probable since the CPS program had not fully satisfied the idealism of the World War II draftees who refused service in the military. The Frankfurt MVS thus worked on a suggested plan and sent the proposal to Executive Secretary O. O. Miller on August 29, 1950.[133]

On December 4, 1950, Miller responded to me indicating that the Executive Committee of MCC had approved the proposal as follows:

> Our December 2 Executive Committee took note of this as per the following minute: Moved and passed to accept the following Executive Secretary's recommendation: that the Committee get ready and stand ready (1) to recruit up to 20 IV-E deferred single men into an European Danziger resettlement builder's unit. . . . [134]

The length of time was for one year on a standard MCC VS basis but with expenses to be borne by the sending congregation.[135] The first Pax unit arrived on April 6, 1951, even before the official beginnings of war with North Korea.[136]

Ironically the Pax idea was implemented before official approval was given by the U.S. Selective Service for conscientious objectors to receive credit for alternative service abroad. MCC and MVS thus launched actions for Selective Service to approve the project. General Lewis B. Hershey, director of Selective Service, made a trip to Europe in 1951 to evaluate the MCC VS program as well as the Church of the Brethren program. Hershey visited several MVS and Church of the Brethren camps, including the Mainz MVS work camp where Walter Eisenbeis and I were camp directors. He was especially interested in the fact that there were several East German girls present at the camp. (See photo, p. 36). Hershey apparently was impressed with the practical organization and accomplishments of the MVS program. Along with the Pax program and the Church of the Brethren VS work, he could foresee COs working in this kind of setting and receiving alternative service credit. He returned to the United States and recommended that alternative service for COs be granted. Truman signed the new agreement in February 1952.[137]

As noted, early Pax operations were parallel and closely connected to the MVS story. A major contingent of the first Pax that arrived in Europe on April 6, 1951, was dispatched to Espelkamp. They moved into poison gas bunkers MVS campers had converted into living quarters for the Pax men. For the first year, the Pax men slept in single army cots three tiers high. The top tier became a premium because it was warmer in the cold nights. The major goal of the Pax program was to help with a major refugee settlement, in cooperation with the German Evangelical Church, and support of the German government.

Pax also expanded the work MVSers had begun among Espelkamp refugees. Creating a crisis, hundreds, probably even thousands, of refugees were arriving in West Germany from "the east" and East Germany every day. After extensive negotiations with the German government, it was agreed that the Pax men would provide the ten percent down payment in the form of building the homes under the supervision of German-appointed superintendents for thousands of refugees who were penniless and had no cash to make the down payment.[138]

In subsequent situations many projects shared personnel and goals. There was extensive interaction and communication between MVS and Pax men. Since I was director of both programs, in the first years, from 1951 to 1952, coordination and cooperation were rather easy. The most flexible and effective program was the quick-response Caravan, described above, which served both organizations. Many Pax men welcomed the chance to leave the more routine work of building homes to join a Caravan project, since it entailed more travel, co-educational campers, and more varied projects.

As already indicated, the MVS camp program continued to be administered in a generally similar fashion under the organization that had slowly evolved. But the context was changing. Europe was on the road to recovery and the emergency character of the needs had began to decrease; this was so especially in Germany which because of the Marshall Plan witnessed the "miracle" of post-World War II European recovery. It is clear that the emergency needs resulting from World War II were being met, and the economies of the other participants in the "great war" were also recovering. The location of the

Above: Caravan, helping with Zeilshiem Germany Church construction,1952. Clockwise, Bim Noe, Holland; Richard Rush, U.S.; Robert Lee, U.S. Courtesy Richard Rush. *Below: MVS Caravan at Holland Flood, 1953.* Courtesy Roger Hochstetler

17 MVS Caravan at Holland Flood, 1953. Courtesy Roger Hochstetler

MVS Caravan volunteers, Holland Flood, 1953. Courtesy Roger Hochstetler

LaMarr Kopp, Nel Boon, Berlin, Germany MVS work camp 1955. Courtesy Nel Kopp

camps shows the gradual decrease in war-torn Germany. The focus then began to shift to other countries with less direct World War II destruction and more community development was emphasized.

In the context of this recovery, young people were beginning to feel the pull of moving into careers and other opportunities and were able to do so with more ease. The volunteers thus began to show more interest in more varied experiences, while the number of urgent projects also diminished.

However, other difficulties began to emerge, partly related to the above factors but not entirely. The urgency of the trauma of World War II and the great stresses of post-war reconstruction had helped transcend the differences between the Mennonite Conferences in France, Germany, Switzerland, and the Netherlands. But with recovery, the work camp movement, which had become established as a central youth program for the European conferences, began to be looked at a bit more critically. And differing perceptions of the appropriateness of the MVS for the European Mennonites began to emerge.

We now turn to the specific history of the formation of the formal MVS organization and its functioning, the troubles it faced, and its being disbanded in 1971.

Warga, Netherlands, MVS camp, 1956. Courtesy Loyal Klassen

Left: Warga, MVS camp, 1956. Courtesy Loyal Klassen

Below: Warga MVS Camp, 1956. Courtesy Loyal Klassen

Chapter 4

THE HISTORY AND FORMATION OF THE MENNONITE VOLUNTARY SERVICE ORGANIZATION

Many observers of human history probably would agree that a successful collective response to a major need or a crisis must become formally and rationally organized. If the need is more than a passing emergency, a rational goal and structure are imperative if the response is to be effective and lasting. The early Christian church illustrates: Acts 6 famously exemplifies this process:

> The twelve called the whole body of disciples together and said, "It would be a grave mistake for us to neglect the word of God to wait at table. Therefore, friends, look out seven men of good reputation from your number and we will appoint them to deal with these matters." (Acts 6:2-3)

And thus church organization began. MCC, which emerged in 1920 to serve a specific and short term crisis in Russia, was a very simple and job-oriented organization. "MCC is an organization which spontaneously grew out of the desire of the Mennonite brotherhood to feed the hungry, clothe the naked, and to testify by loving service to the gospel of peace and service."[139] But as time went on, MCC took on more long-range challenges and thus faced the process of "rationalization" to be effective, so that at present it is an impressive organization with global reach. "The Mennonite Central Committee has grown into the largest inter-Mennonite organization in the world, with a vast variety of organizational relationships and program involvements."[140]

The emerging MCC voluntary service organization must now be placed in the larger historical context of American-European Mennonite relationships, which will expand the understanding of the emergence of the Mennonite Voluntary Service vision and the direction it actually took—as well as its demise. Most American Mennonites trace their religious and ethnic origins to Europe and Russia. As is well known, almost universally, the emigrants' relations with the sending community tends to languish with time. The literature on ethnicity is peopled with "first, second, and third" generations and their relationships with the "home country."

So it was with the American Mennonites, who began to develop their own traditions in the "New World," from the days of the earliest immigrations. World Wars I and II helped the weakening and separation of bonds of the two groups. In addition to the alienation caused by World War II, there was considerable distance, even mistrust between the European Mennonites and the Americans for a variety of reasons beginning already in the nineteenth century. Differences between the American Mennonites and the European Mennonite conferences were due largely to their slowly divergent cultural histories.[141]

Though the differences cannot be fully described here, they include the following: the Swiss, French, and South German Mennonites had become more pietist than the Dutch; hence the Dutch were considered "too liberal"by the other groups; on the other hand, the German Mennonites were criticized by the other groups because of their alleged nationalism and support of Hitler and Nazi Germany's policies. (These attitudes of course was not uniformly held by the various Mennonite congregations in Germany.)

World War II was however a major cause for increasing divergencies, especially in theology. Thus Harold S. Bender states, "The two serious world wars (1914- and 1940-45) together with the rise of communism in Russia, have had divisive effects on Mennonitism in Europe." These conflicts "seriously alienated the French and Swiss Mennonites from the Germans, [and caused] even greater alienation between the Dutch and the Germans."[142] They obviously also hurt the trust of American Mennonites.

These factors plus others were thus at work and affected the development of the voluntary service program in Europe. Though the "official" work camp efforts of the American volunteers focused more on the immediate impacts of World War II, almost from their beginnings the American participants in the camps were interested in engaging the European young people, especially the Mennonite youth, and convincing them of pacifism and the way of peace. The European Mennonites generally, including the youth, did not fully trust the Americans, especially in their "cavalier" attitude regarding the universality of the nonresistant position.[143]

The European campers, again including Mennonite youth, believed that the Americans did not understand what it meant to live under ideological totalitarian conditions and war. However, the Europeans in general, having experienced so much emergency relief assistance, sympathy, and encouragement through the American MCC and other church organizations, did not want to openly challenge or disagree with the Americans. The young people, including MVS campers, reflected this attitude. There is little doubt that the American MCC personnel in general, including the American work campers, exuded a self-confidence that offended the Europeans, but the latter could not openly express this feeling.[144]

The first conference evaluating the MVS summer work camps in 1950 turned out to be a crucial event for the emergence of the MVS idea and its formation in Europe. The meeting took place August 28, 1950, at Thomashof, in Baden Wuertemberg.[145] The meeting was originally

> intended to be an all-day meeting where the leaders of
> the various camps, plus camper representatives the

leaders chose, were to express the sentiment of their camp in all the varying angles of its life.

It was assumed MCC could use the ideas for future planning to make the camps all the more effective. The evaluations were very candid and meaningful; everyone was convinced that the work camp idea was a modern form of witness and service.[146]

After the respective conference representatives from the four countries in Europe had heard the various reports and discussion, a summary report of the conference concluded,

> These men [sic] were all enthusiastic about this new line of action and pledged their support. They asked us to prepare a memo they could present to their own church conferences when they met in their fall sessions.[147]

It was with increasing awareness of this environment that MCC staff gently tried to more fully involve European Mennonites in the voluntary service work and to invite them to participate in administering it. There were of course already numerous interactions between MCC staff and European Mennonite lay people and persons in official positions from the time MCC entered Europe. But the enthusiastic involvement of Mennonite youth in the voluntary service activities soon demanded a "rationalizing" for their managerial involvement.

This led to formation of an MVS advisory council with representatives from each of the four countries—France, Germany, Holland, and Switzerland—in summer 1950. The memo of understanding for the proposed European Voluntary Service was composed and sent the following day (Aug. 29) to the invited representatives from the four countries, who presented the plan to their respective official conferences. The proposal

> requested that each country elect a representative to a V.S. council, which council was to get acquainted with the V.S. concept, and program, being responsible for the interpretation and promotion of the work, and gradually taking charge of the program within their respective countries.[148]

The churches responded very favorably; by October 1, all but one country had elected its representative. "These repre-

sentatives had no special commission from their home conference and together we had to slowly and painfully plot our aims
and course of action."[149] A meeting of the new International
Mennonite Voluntary Service Council was held on December
29 and 30, 1950, and continued at the Frankfurt MCC office.

> The first meeting took place Friday evening at the con-
> clusion of the campers reunion held from the 27th to the
> 29th at Ruedesheim. The representatives attended the
> reunion because it was thought that they would be able
> to experience first hand a little of the spirit that pervades
> youth work in the European theater. There was unani-
> mous and enthusiastic opinion that the Voluntary Ser-
> vice movement was very much worth while and essen-
> tial.[150]

The discussion included a review of MCC's work camp activities, the developing refugee settlement program, and reflections on the possibilities of some American young fellows coming to help in the refugee resettlement, the possibilities of having European youth serve in these programs and even participate in the alternative service dimension, and the request that
the European representatives be kept fully informed of all developments. The decision was made that MCC Frankfurt VS office would be responsible for administering the program that
the council approved and that the staff should

> start immediately a campaign for volunteers in the
> churches and for financial support for the work, this
> campaign to be discharged through personal appear-
> ances and films depicting the work.[151]

The final actions at this meeting were—

> That the new International Mennonite Voluntary Ser-
> vice organization be called *MENNONITISCHER FREI-
> WILLIGENDIENST* [Mennonite Voluntary Service].
> Further action indicated that the inscription and symbol
> be printed in the language of each country, that the sym-
> bol be the cross with clasped hands and that the Frank-
> furt office take the initiative in implementing these deci-
> sions.[152] Even though the representatives admitted that

they were not [yet] approved by all the churches in their respective countries, they nevertheless were the official delegates who justified the decisions made here.[153]

To discuss proposed vision further, the representatives from the four countries were invited to meet at Espelkamp, where they could also visit the newly implemented Pax refugee housing construction project. The representatives were amazed at what they saw being done and were even more enthused about the nature of the voluntary service project. The project, the refugee housing the American young men in Pax were constructing, "made the council members see their responsibility and they determined to arouse interest and support in their own country" for the VS vision.[154]

The representatives from three of the four countries and two MCC staff members who stayed at Espelkamp on April 9 and 10, 1951, produced a "Provisional Constitution" for the vision and the goals of the proposed European Mennonite Voluntary Service work.[155] The purposes and vision were expressed as follows: 1) generate Christian service to alleviate the serious needs in the European communities; 2) provide opportunities for Mennonite Youth of Mennonite Congregations to serve the above needs; 3) give a Christian witness through the work, through contact with other participants of the work camps, and through members of the communities in which they served.[156]

The structure of the organization and guidelines included the following: 1) the representative from each country was to serve as promoter of the program; 2) retain close contact with the youth for encouragement and nurture; 3) locate and sponsor projects in each country; 4) promote relationships with other work camp organizations and potential campers in countries where Mennonites did not exist; 5) locate work projects in other lands where such work needs to be done; 6) remain in contact with former volunteers for continuing nurture.[157] The representatives from the four countries were encouraged to nurture enthusiasm and support for the vision and program.

In the meantime, another result of the enthusiasm for the results of the work camp experience was the creation of a "deputation team" to promote VS in the Mennonite congregations. At the suggestion of Samuel Gerber of Switzerland, a voluntary service team was created whose purpose was to inform the Swiss Mennonite churches about the nature of the voluntary service program and its witness and service opportunities as well as the refugee problem and how the Swiss churches could contribute to solving this problem.

Seven churches in the Jura area were visited. A slide show describing the tremendous need in Germany was presented along with slides depicting life in the camp. If it was successful, similar tours were proposed for the other countries. "The publicity tour of the Swiss churches [which] took place on November 5-14 resulted in enough money for Sam Gerber to cover his expenses of 1951."[158]

In addition to the Swiss tour, a tour of French churches took place on February 24 to March 3, 1951, resulting in a budget for MFD in France and a contribution to the secretariat. "Germany is setting up a yearly budget and has already contributed to the MFD general expenses." The congregational response in Switzerland was overwhelmingly positive. Gerber was enthused (*Begeistert*) and exclaimed, "This was probably the first organized and concerted effort to mobilize the youth for such a worthwhile cause [in Switzerland]" at an MVS council meeting.[159] He also suggested that this type of congregational visit should be carried out in all the European countries.[160] His emerging positive mood was reflected by Bob Lee, a staffer with extensive MVS experience in early 1952:

> In the past year, the concept of voluntary service has become more generally accepted and approved by the European Mennonite circles; consequently the MVS work camp idea was further developed and expanded to serve the needs of the youth and to alleviate the distress of the suffering [people]. These opportunities of service arising from Europe's tremendous post-war problems, provided a challenge to Christian brotherly love and to the Mennonite testimony of peace and nonresistance. Here a positive witness of love and peace could be demonstrated in both word and deed.[161]

Enthusiasm for these deputations was not matched with continued implementation, for no further tours in this format took place for the next several years, though there were reunions in various places and times thereafter. The establishment of an European MVS program was on its way. But the need for financing of the new organization was high on the agenda. At the April 9, 1951, meeting at Espelkamp the agenda included "the relation of MFD to the youth groups in other countries, the guiding principles in choosing camp projects, the question of having an European representative in the secretariat, and financing."[162]

The concern that Europeans begin to take more ownership was raised by MCC.

> MCC asked the question whether a [sic] European should not be brought into the secretaryship [sic]. Therewith the European participation would be strengthened and enlarged. Possibilities were mentioned, Rene Peterschmitt, Alsace, France, Wolfgang Fieguth, Deutschland, and Daniel Habegger, Switzerland. The committee [asked] to think about this further.[163]

The financing problem continued to be a concern at subsequent meetings but there was no clear direction on this topic.

> There was little to discuss as far as finances were concerned. A central treasury is being prepared but its relation to MCC must be cleared. [The council] is working toward the idea that each account shall provide financially for its representatives in the camps as much as is necessary [possible]. For the long-term VS workers, there would also have to be spending money.[164]

The financial aspect continued to challenge the council and was not satisfactorily solved for some years.

There was, however, from the beginning of the MVS endeavor an awareness that American know-how and power might not be fully accepted by the European Mennonites or by Europeans in general. So the MVS office in Frankfurt launched a study of some of the responses of local beneficiaries and participants in all the work camps conducted by the fall of 1950. The team was composed of MCCers Norma Jost, Marjorie Yoder, and me.

The responses were generally positive, but the report also included several rather stringent comments. This one was by a Mennonite pastor:

First one would have to say that you MCC people are rather naive. Part of it springs from your arrogant sense of superiority. You forget that we have been living in the Boiling Pot of human relations for thousands of years longer than you have. You come, rent a house and go to work.

This fact describes accurately the way MCC bought the Vogtstrasse 44 house and began the MVS program.

Then the pastor continued:

Even if we cannot do much [financially] we still could possibly help in finding a suitable place [work camp] and enlist all the cooperation possible. There is this eventuality, that regardless of how badly we need your help, if we are not consulted and informed, we will develop a negative attitude and expect you to do all the work. So please, if you start another community center or old people's home [project], let us in on it too. Are we your guests in our own home?[165]

MCC staff in Europe of course had been rather deeply conscious of the uneven distribution of power way by which the entire program was conducted in Europe. But it was not as significant in the earlier emergency period, where the program by definition was basically one type of activity. But in the VS program, where MCC expected cooperation and support, not only in personnel but also in decision-making, the inequality began to be more apparent. The survey tended to elucidate this issue and all the more pushed the VS personnel to "indigenize" the vision as soon as possible.

Thus a dilemma began to emerge: Leadership, vision, and finances were precarious, since MCC did not have unlimited resources, especially for a program which was not as pressing as the refugee problem. Yet such resources were not forthcoming from the Europeans. Hence I wrote to MCC Executive Secretary O. O. Miller,

Of course, the problem we always have [in providing leadership for the summer camps] is the shifting personnel. The difficulty is that when a new program is planned, if there are not a number of people at some place or another who [can be] shifted around, we have no leadership on which to depend. At the present it appears that we have only one or possibly two workers who would be able to make such an arrangement. We are trying to draw in European Mennonite youth who have been in America and others who are eager and waiting, but we still cannot leave the complete direction in European hands [due to lack of experience and financing]. At any rate, next summer's work camps will call for at least six capable American young fellows and girls.[166]

The idea of developing a cadre of VSers who would be flexible and available to serve on various short- and longer-term bases which would help establish the MVS vision was beginning to jell and became the first appeal for personnel for beginning what soon became the MVS Caravan, described above.

Another goal of such a group was to involve war refugees since it enabled them to help themselves, rather than to simply wait for government help.

We hope to have a continuous core of fellows from Holland, Switzerland, France and Germany numbering from 15 to 20 which may vary according to the season. This team (or teams) will be concerned directly with helping the refugee settlement programs which brothers Graber and Klassen are launching. [This team] would not only help the refugees build homes, but be a means to include in the construction work many of the refugees who should be given responsibility in procuring their homes.[167]

The letter suggested that American young fellows of draft age be included in this project, which later became the Pax resettlement program.[168] This movement is illustrated by occasional weekend work camps implemented in relative proximity to the MVS office in Frankfurt which provided opportunity

Warga MVS Work camps: from right, Loyal Klassen; Richard Hertzler, MVS board; Ervin Goering, earlier MVS director; and sixth from right, LaMarr Kopp, director. Courtesy Loyal Klassen

for persons who had regular employment but who were looking for opportunities to participate during free weekends or short vacation times.

However, the idea of continuing longer-term voluntary service projects was beginning to gain momentum. This long-term voluntary service camp idea had its Mennonite precedent at Espelkamp, which was begun in December 1948, and continued in changing forms to the present. However the new emphasis was for a more flexible format, depending on the nature of the project and the availability of volunteers.

The MVS program continued along this trajectory and expanded its reach and depth. In the fall of 1952, as the first director, I informed the council that I wished to return to the United States in December 1952. A search for an European director was launched, and the council suggested a number of names, but none seemed to work out. Richard Hertzler, the council member for Germany, suggested that this might be the time to have the European Mennonites commit to become responsible for the selection of a director and for the financial obligations.

After some discussion, the council concluded that this idea was not feasible, so the council appealed to me to extend my term for another year, but my immediate future plans did not allow me to accept the invitation. An interim appointment of a Dutch camper, Jan de Vries, seemed to be the best solution for the moment, and he accepted the appointment as director.[169]

Jan de Vries served from January 1953 to May 15, 1954, when LaMarr Kopp from the U.S. became director. As implied above, part of the dynamic for appointing an American was the financial aspect of the program. Since MCC was a major contributor to the cost of the MVS program, it was a problematic for MCC to support a European in the position if the Europeans were not going to assume financial responsibilities. In a letter to the European MVS council on December 10 shortly before my departure, European director H. A. Fast wrote,

> You will realize that up to this point, MCC has carried the burden and the other groups [the European Mennonite conferences] have simply made occasional contributions. Now the understanding is that the European Mennonite youth groups carry the major financial re-

*Above: Warga
Work camp,
progress of MVS
campers at work.*
Courtesy Loyal
Klassen

*Left: Tsakones,
Greece, work
camp, 1962.*
Courtesy Nelson
Good

sponsibility, and MCC can be counted on to contribute their share. You will understand, therefore, that it is rather urgent, that we have immediate word from you, informing us what you propose to do as far as your group is concerned. We must at least furnish Jan [de Vries] with information from where support is coming from, and what he can count on.[170]

Had the European Mennonites been able (and willing?) to carry a majority of the costs, likely the entire MVS program might have become more indigenous early on and entrenched itself in the psyche of the European Mennonites. In light of the many difficulties discussed above, one set of factors indicates the dilemmas of the venture, namely the support source and length of term and hence the nationality of the directors.

Clearly, in case the director was an American MCC appointee, the person was loaned to the MVS program, whereas the Europeans who would serve as directors would be heavily subsidized by MCC. As will emerge in subsequent pages, with the gradual decline in the importance and salience of the work camp movement, the European Mennonites had not "bought into" the program enough by the time the interest began to flag.[171] But MCC, not wanting to see the program terminate, continued to supply strong leadership and the majority of the financing, with little success.

The MVS program developed in the general trajectory envisioned from its beginnings. However, some of the work camps, such as the ones in 1953 in the flooded areas of Holland (Oudorp and Nieuwe Tonge) and two camps in Austria and two in Germany, were continuing camps. The Caravan and other weekend and special projects were more experimental and were created in response to specific needs. In these camps, as has been indicated above at various places, MVS worked with the Pax program in providing alternative service opportunities for volunteers. This had been the vision from the beginning. Thus in 1954, the *MVS Newsletter* reported,

MVS has made history. With the arrival of four English COs sent by the Friends Ambulance Unit (FAU) there are now COs [from] three countries working at

Dreischor. In October the three types of COs were: Mennonite I-Ws, better known as Pax boys, a Dutch Mennonite who is the first to be drafted to work outside government camps, and the FAU. We also have a Brethren Voluntary service worker.[172]

The MVS camp at Dreichor, in the province of Zeeland, had special significance for the MVS program, because of the presence of Dutch COs who were hoping to get Dutch recognition for alternative service: A law entitled the "Law on Refusal of Military Service" was passed in 1924 which "offered the first alternative civilian service in the Netherlands. They were given a choice of performing alternative civilian service that would last a year longer than the military service of regular conscripts."[173] The accepted projects had until that point not included Mennonite work camps; it is not clear whether he got credit for his service with MVS.[174]

Above: Graz, Austria, MVS work camp, 1961. Below: Worms, Germany, MVS work camp, 1961. Both photos courtesy Nelson Good

Left: Lamastre, France, MVS work camp, 1961. Right: Hermon , France, MVS work camp, 1963. Both photos courtesy Jaap Rem

Chapter 5

THE TRANSFORMATION AND TERMINATION OF MENNONITE VOLUNTARY SERVICE

Considering the number of camp projects, the work accomplished, and the number of young people who participated and were changed, one would conclude that the European Mennonite Voluntary Service had been an unqualified success. The impact of the camp experience on the campers, the leaders, the sending communities both European and American, and the recipient communities has been overwhelmingly documented and widely recognized. It would be redundant to parade all the accomplishments and the testimonials again. Why then did this program, which functioned with such enthusiasm, spirit, and achievements, suddenly terminate?

Part of the reason was, as indicated above, that emergency conditions of post-World War II Europe had dramatically improved. Material needs were receding into the background as the European countries returned to a more tranquil life, largely assisted by the Marshall Plan. But persistent concerns and even doubts began to be more vocally expressed. At first the concerns appeared to be economic—why were the European Mennonite sponsoring groups not forthcoming enough in their support? In June 1955, after LaMarr Kopp had been executive director for about a year, he wrote to MCC Executive Secretary O. O. Miller:

> It is quite obvious that I have failed in my work. I was sent to Europe to do the work of a liaison worker: to develop a program [which would become "owned" by the European Mennonites but] which to some Europeans seems particularly American in ideology, largely supported by American money. The MVS program is little or no closer to the European Mennonites than it was before. Now that an American has taken over, MVS will move on somehow. Only we must be careful of this idea of "bigness" and expansion, and of course pacifism "seems to be the thinking."[175]

Kopp continues,

> Both Kauffman and I were unhappily impressed during the council meeting at the attitude of the Council toward the support of our program. Very frankly, there seems to be the general feeling that from America will come any help or support we need. Americans have money, why should they not give?[176]

The issue seemed to be financial, as noted above. But apparently other issues were under the surface, for just before Kopp returned to the United States, he concluded his December 7 letter to Miller by suggesting that the MVS council would like Miller to speak to a ministers' conference on the challenges of MVS. Kopp states that "One wonders whether Switzerland and France were not much happier without the burden of MVS. On the other hand, the reception of MVS in Holland is most gratifying, and to hear, as I did recently, a Dutch pastor say, "We need MVS; our young people need MVS."[177]

But another type of concern, implying a need for a clearer statement of objectives and operating regulations of MVS, began to emerge. In April 29, 1959, apparently at the request of the MVS council, MVS Executive Secretary Erwin C. Goering wrote to the MVS council, "Enclosed you will find a copy of the only semblance of a constitution which MVS possesses to date.

This apparently was drawn up very early, near the beginning of MVS, and has not been reworked since." Goering advised the council to study the document, and come to the next meeting, scheduled for July 4, where "it would be well to discuss the reworking of the constitution. MVS [has now] developed to the place where I think it needs a definite working constitution which can be our guide."[178]

The first specific documented uneasiness with the MVS work camp organization and work came from the French Mennonite Church. A four-page, single-spaced paper sent to LaMar Reichert in November was signed by the three persons representing French Youth Commission, Willy Peterschmitt, Ernest Hege, and Max Schowalter. The paper begins: "MVS has repeatedly asked whether the French Mennonite Youth organization might not become an official supporter of MVS. It was suggested that MVS would provide an opportunity for our young people to give a positive Christian witness "[179] The introduction suggests that occasionally individual French young people had participated but a general response from the conference encouraging participation did not ensue. "In this paper, we would like to explain our reluctance to officially support MVS."[180]

The paper began by stating that the French young people were basically rural and needed on the farms. Further, the costs of participating in the camps could be prohibitive. More to the point, the paper suggested that the French Mennonite youth were rural in orientation, not acquainted or conversant with the "urban" culture. They would thus not be able to stand up for their convictions in the open and free interaction and discussion prevalent in the work camp structure and might themselves be tempted to compromise their faith:

> We are deeply concerned that our young people would not obtain sufficient spiritual guidance in the camps. Hence we are convinced that we should encourage our young people to participate in Bible schools and Bible camps, rather than MVS.[181]

On January 12, LaMar Reichert replied to Willy Peterschmitt, Ernest Hege, Max Showalter, and Jean-Jacques Hirschy:

We thank you for your paper stating your position regarding MVS, even though it was not very good news for us. We are very regretful that the French High Commission could not evaluate our work in a more positive light.

Reichert then states that the position paper will stir increased attempts to meet the concerns of the French. He continues somewhat testily,

We truly [*Tatsaechlich*] have seen our mission till the present moment, to express our faith in the world in the best sense of the Word [of God]. We wanted thereby to let the young persons, who came from a variety of backgrounds and nationalities, know that a Christian can truly be joyful and energetically witness to his faith.

Reichert then concludes: "We truly think [though] that the work camp is still a crucial place where youth could experience Christian life and witness."[182]

The Swiss Mennonites shared considerable concerns with the French Mennonites, but no official statement parallel to that of the French was apparently ever presented. The German and Dutch Mennonites were more favorable to the work camp idea and its accomplishments and more supportive of MVS both in personnel and finances. However, there were regional differences. The North German *Vereinigung* tended to reflect the more liberal Dutch while the south German *Verband* tended to align with the more orthodox or evangelical orientation of the French and the Swiss Mennonites of the south of Europe.

This situation was extensively stated in a three-page, single-spaced letter from Hans Jacob Galle, the German representative on the MVS board, to Abram Braun, a longtime pillar in the *Konference der Sueddeutschen Mennoniten*. He asks for help in convincing the German Mennonites to more strongly support the MVS program:

It has been difficult for me to represent both organizations, since I get so little indication of support or direction from either. Probably the main question that faced the M.V.S. board at our last meeting is whether it has a unique role to play in the light of the many other organizations that are existing today. We believe that it does have a unique role, namely to provide our young people with an opportunity to serve the needy and through word and deed to express our faith in Christ.[183]

Galle continues by asking Braun to wield his influence to obtain the commitment of the German Mennonites to more actively support the MVS with financial support. He proposes that in the light of the improvement of Mennonites economically, "we finally begin to take more financial responsibility in supporting the MVS program."[184] The financial concerns as well as the theological issues continued to hover over the organization, however. Even though there are no indications in the *MVS Newsletters* and other published documents that there were major difficulties or tensions, the end was approaching.

Nevertheless MVS reunions took place in various countries in which the ex-campers came to be reunited with friends and to reminisce about the good times the camps had provided. Usually MVS office personnel participated. Thus the reunion on November 6-7, 1965, at Amersfoort, the Netherlands, included looking at slides that various persons had taken in camp. This gave the individual an opportunity to express his views and experiences as well giving everyone an idea as to how other camps were realized. The notes concluded that "All 12 MVS work camps of the past summer were represented. I cannot help but be impressed by the attendance and organizational set-up as well as the project which we accomplished."[185]

In 1969, some changes were made which in retrospect seem to indicate coming difficulties. The September 1969 *MVS Newsletter* stated that Isert was returning to Canada and that Hans-Joachim Wienss from Enkenbach, Germany, would become the new director. The statement indicated that Wienss brought many fine qualities that would be beneficial in carrying on the work of MVS. Before beginning his assignment as MVS director, he had earlier participated in numerous voluntary service projects, including MVS.[186]

The September 1969 issue also included an article by Joerg Isert on "Twenty Years of Voluntary Service," which began "With joy and thanksgiving we look back at this time to the last 20 years. The blessings received were many whether to those who were helped or to the work campers themselves."[187] The article then reviewed briefly MCC postwar relief and rehabilitation services and suggested that the work camps were mounted to help in rebuilding projects, especially in Germany. Many volunteers served in a variety of projects and "as the physical needs became less relevant, MVS expanded into a new work of social concern. This led to the organization in 1961 of the long-term service program at a Protestant Institution in West Berlin" (*Johannesstift*)[188].

Isert reviews the dramatic increase in interest for the work camps and the projects, so that

> today, MVS organizes camps in 7-9 different countries, including Israel. Volunteers come from 15-20 countries and 4 continents. Our latest plans are to recruit and assign qualified volunteers for service in developing countries. This again will be in cooperation with American Mennonites who presently have workers in about 35 countries.

Isert concludes by thanking the "many who have helped to make MVS what it is today. We will continue, as in the past, with our efforts to work in the Spirit of Jesus Christ." The concluding reference to working in the "Spirit of Jesus Christ" was not uniformly expressed in earlier communications and *Newsletters* and may indicate that there was some background against which this language was used.

In the second last paragraph of the article Isert reflects on the purpose of MVS.

> What remains is the purpose of the work. Christian convictions motivated the volunteer to a service for Christ. This service was obvious as long as homes for refugees had to be built and destroyed churches rebuilt. Today's work campers do not always see directly the help they give people. It is only after some reflection that one can see where help has been given, even in building a parking lot in a Christian institution of a large city—the aim remains the same—to build bridges of understanding and to be a peace witness in today's world.[189]

In the December 1969 *Newsletter*, Wienss, the new MVS director, wrote a one-page article, "Reflections." He asks, "What have we done in the year 1969 to help eliminate the needs of the world and aid our fellowmen?" (sic). He suggests that it must be said "in all fairness that there have been successes, failures, accomplishments, and frustrations. How can we then best fulfill the tasks which we have been asked to undertake?" He expresses thanks to all the volunteers for their generous service: "Your willingness to serve and to help with the ongoing work of MVS has greatly been appreciated by the MVS staff."[190]

The plans for the 1970 year were routinely publicized, and fifteen camps were conducted. But the concerns about the purpose of the European voluntary service program were getting louder. The issues regarding the future of MVS began to be more intensively discussed in the ensuing months. In the March 1970 issue, Jaap Rem, a Dutch volunteer and retiring MVS director, reiterated some of the matters in play in an article on "Your Help Is Needed." He reported that "The disparities between the rich and poor are no longer accepted by young people." Rem continued,

> Many older people are in acquiescence with all kinds of political and economic systems. Unfortunately too many are too concerned about their well-paid jobs rather than with the work of voluntary services. However, there are many ways to change the mentality of the people, to make a positive and Christian contribution, and improve the situation in this world—go to a work camp!

Rem listed four ways in which work camps contributed to the goals of MVS, including being "willing to adapt ourselves to the local situations where work camps are located, and to give ourselves in Christian services to mankind."[191] It is clear that the interests of the volunteers were leaning more toward changing the world, while the supporting Mennonite conferences were increasingly concerned about the "religious and spiritual" character of the program.

Thus in the June 1970 *MVS Newsletter*, Reverend Peter Foth, of the Hamburg Mennonite Church, offered an analysis of the challenges of MVS, entitled "What Really Counts Is the 'Action.'" He opens by stating, "When one is asked to put something down on paper about the meaning, goals and tasks of an MVS work camp, I have decided it is not as simple as it at first appears." Foth then zeroes in on the word *action*. "The emphasis of our day is that the 'word' can sometimes be omitted but the 'action' never. MVS camps, without a doubt, belong to the category of 'action.'" Foth avers that "with the Mennonite faith went the deed and speaking, as well as thoughts and faith. One might call it 'Active Faith.'"

Foth asks why people join MVS. Is it for personal advancement, experience, self satisfaction, to help, to be a witness, to expand our faith and transform it into action? All of these motives are operative, Foth declares in conclusion:

> MVS camps are actions, usually with, sometimes without explanatory [explaining] words. Why do we go to camps? Because they are timely and modern, because they are suitable for our faith and to our word. Because they give us the opportunity to bring together that which is often separated or stands irrelatively [sic] side by side: "Faith and Life."[192]

This treatise was obviously judiciously crafted by a sympathetic minister to bridge the gap between the young people's interests and demands and the supporting Mennonite churches. "Action" without a clearly stated religious testimony and witness to accompany the action was at the heart of the unrest in the supporting congregations, especially in France and Switzerland. The MVS staff and presumably MCC, which represented a generally more progressive position, were struggling to keep the work camp movement thriving. Ironically at the height of the number of camps conducted, and the number of volunteers involved, the threats of dissolution were growing.

A changed environment was at hand: The physical, economic, and social dislocations of the "great war" were beginning to recede. In addition the "youth rebellion" of the late '60s and early '70s was in its formative stages. The sponsoring Mennonite conferences were not ready for the challenges. In the next *MVS Newsletter*, September 1970, the new MVS director wrote an essay entitled "Looking Back." Wienss proposed that MVS workers in the office as well as all those who participate in camps [needed to] "look back to the camp season in a critical but honest way. After an honest evaluation, we can draw conclusions for our future work and make it possible for constructive continuation in our work."

Wienss proposed "two essentials" concerning this work:. "our church background as Mennonites and the basis of our work as Christians linked to that background [and] to encounter with young people in our camps."[193] He reminded his readers that the volunteers of the day

> are different from those one met in the past war camps [sic]. Schelsky called them the skeptic generation. The following generation in North America as well as in Western Europe saw a sweet economical boom and became lazy. In the last few years, many young people in our Western societies, particularly students, have become strict critics of the establishment—they are rather disappointed by the bitter aftertaste of the sweet boom. Because they have been disappointed by the distorting forms and insignificant ways of speaking the meet in state, society and church.[194]

Thus Wienss believed they were disillusioned and rejected the values of their parents and were looking for a more meaningful and more righteous life. Further he stated that the churches had disappointed these young people with their insignificant sermons with regard to the significance of the individual.

In light of this situation, he proposed that in MVS

> we have been trying to express and emphasize the guide lines of our work with young people. Perhaps here or there we have been using empty forms and have been speaking in insignificant terms. [But] in our work we have been trying to honestly and seriously make visible this gospel of Jesus which is relevant to us. Is this news of Jesus, no longer contemporary? Probably we have to fine new possibilities to express our concerns as Chris-

tians, to express our concerns for man, the individual as well as "man individual in society" to stand up for real righteousness in man's life in our world today.

Wienss then referred to the second item people meeting people in the camps.

Some thought it was good, others were disappointed. How do we face each other, how do we meet, how do we act in front of each other? Refusal, antipathy, forming cliques or acceptance of each other and honest interest in the fellow man? Perhaps also forgiveness and reconciliation?

The article concludes with a quote from Peter J. Dyck, European MCC director:

The key word in witnessing is not "action" but "interaction." Without interaction of one person with another, there can be no communication, hence no helping the other man. It is in the implementation of a truly comprehensive ministry which includes both word and deed that we are currently most vulnerable and need retooling if we are going to be obedient to our Lord and enable him to work more effectively through us.[195]

Then in March 1971, the sky fell in with this terse announcement:

Dear Friends, This *MVS Newsletter* will be rather surprising for you and we ask for your insight and understanding. At the beginning of this year, the council of Mennonite Voluntary Service had taken the decision to terminate the volunteer program this coming June after more than 20 years. A thoughtful reflection of the last years activities and their tendencies had led to this decision.

The notice, written by director Hans-Joachim Wienss, provided the reasons:

Within the recent years there has been a diverging tendency noticeable as to the MVS goals on one side and the motivation of our volunteers on the other side. Our aims in general were to do a meaningful work at a project as well as to give a common expression of Christian belief. We felt that in particular the latter hardly could be fulfilled anymore.

He suggested that an alternative to the short term, "traditional pick and shovel work [is not feasible]; we have to have an alternative. There will be talks with friends to evaluate possibilities of another type of service."[196]

Some concluding observations by Wienss, the last director of MVS, provide philosophical and theological observations concerning the final termination of MVS:

MVS aims and goals were all known by the volunteers; however they looked at these guidelines in different ways, which is a natural thing to do. On the other hand we stated that most volunteers accepted the way the groups were led. We met devoted young Christian people and people who were open to discuss and reflect on the biblical message. They sat in with the group when we had devotional gatherings as well as speeches given on Mennonite history and Anabaptist topics as were those on conscientious objection and nonresistance. Yet there were folks who were not willing to even listen, but practiced "so-to say" obstructions. More and more the last couple of years we met this type of young people. And often it was rather difficult for camp leaders to follow our guidelines.[197]

Wienss analyzes some of the reasons for this "obstructionist attitude" in the context of the more general cultural shift taking place in Europe and in the West in general. He suggests that on the basis of the social milieu in Western Europe at the time,

Students at colleges and universities used discussion more and more to show opposition and obstruction. Discussion had become an instrument to say "no" to [present] programs, attitudes, institutions. Accepted structures and values were questioned and rejected. Also a general aspect of change came into play as to the traditional pick and shovel work of VS groups In MVS in particular we sensed that the Christian aspects of doing voluntary service and relating to each other had been looked at as not relevant.

Wienss concludes, "The pick and shovel period in western Europe had come to an end, the 'rebuilding' after the war was done. Another generation had proclaimed their idea of 're-building a society.'"

As the dissolution was taking place alternatives were being explored. In the Netherlands, for example, a "Friends of Eirene" group had been formed, as reported in the January 3, 1970, issue of the *Algemene Doopsgesinde Weekblad*.[198] Its purpose was to inform young people of the possibilities of service under Eirene and encourage dialogue concerning world needs. The December 12, 1970, issue noted that Eirene had projects in seven locations in Morocco.

To provide some possibilities for summer service in 1971, the *Newsletter* stated, "Since Mennonite Voluntary Service is no longer organizing summer work camps, we would like to draw your attention to MCC Summer Service . . . Akron Pennsylvania . . . if you live in North America; or to Ecumenical Youth Service . . . Switzerland if you live in Europe."[199] They also encouraged young people to join Eirene.

Notices were placed in the Mennonite periodicals of the supporting countries. Thus in the official Dutch weekly a brief announcement entitled "Greetings MVS" stated that the "MVS work camps have had their day. The time was twenty years. Thousands of young people from all over the world have given help to their neighbors." However, the readers were reminded that "with the end of MVS this type of help is not at an end. These Mennonites belonged to the pioneers. In a different and broader form, this work will be continued."[200]

In Germany the *Mennonitisches Jahrbuch* for 1972 stated that

MFD [MVS] has terminated its voluntary service program after 23 years of existence. Two basic issues brought the supporting council of MCC, France, Germany, Switzerland, and the Netherlands to this decision after a critical analysis: First, no successor was found for Hans-Joachim Wienss to carry on the work. Secondly we concluded that there was a very clear cleavage between the goals of MVS and the motivation of the volunteers who came to the camps.[201]

As the MVS program was coming to a close, other compensatory actions were beginning to take shape. The Dutch and German Mennonites had begun cooperating in IMO (*Internationale Mennonitische Organisation*) and cooperated with MCC for foreign service programs in 1967.[202] Development volunteers were sent to numerous countries, including Paraguay, Uruguay, Nicaragua, Guatemala, India, Chad, and refuge camps in Europe.[203] The *Jaarboekje* for 1971 states that one volunteer had been sent to Paraguay via IMO. In 1973, two volunteers were sent to Haiti, another to Israel, and a fourth to Paraguay, also under IMO.

The original European MVS program was thus transformed. Volunteers from Germany and Netherlands were at first channeled through the new IMO. "Short term work camps . . . were organized by the 'Jugendwerk' of the South German Mennonite Conference." Klaus Huebert was instrumental in

> making [the former] MVS useful for the work with Mennonite youth in south Germany. So he had the idea to somehow integrate the short term voluntary service idea of the terminated program into his work with the Mennonite youth, or add this aspect of service to it.[204]

However, at the Mennonite World Conference in 1984, the German delegation urged the formation of a new voluntary service program in Europe. But there was no strong response, so the German Mennonites formally organized the *Christliche Dienste* (CD) in 1986. The governing board (*Traegerkreis*) was made up of representatives from the supporting church organizations including the mission board, the *Mennonitische Hilfswerk Cristenflicht* (MHC), the peace committee, and the youth organization. Each of these organizations were authorized to provide financial help to the CD, and the volunteers in the program were also asked to pay a fee according to a formula which covered the costs not supplied by German Church or voluntary contributions.[205]

The German Christliche Dienste has grown and prospered. By 1996, a total of 269 volunteers had served under CD. The length of service averaged one year and four months. Since 1989, CD has gained recognition to assign German COs for their alternative service term. The applications for service have increased steadily. The religious origin of the volunteers have included Mennonites (some 48 percent); the rest have been Catholics, Lutheran, Reformed, Baptist, and other groups. Nationalities have also reflected something of the earlier MVS, with Germany sending 14.5 percent, the rest of Europe 22.7 percent, South America, 27.1 percent, Africa, 3.3 percent, Asia 5.6 percent, North America, 26.8 percent. Volunteers have served in programs in Paraguay, Brasil, Bolivia, Uruguay, Nicaragua, Guatemala, India, Chad, and refugee settlements in Europe.[206]

After the termination of MVS the Dutch Mennonites also continued sporadic camps, led by Jaap Brusewitz. For a few years Dutch volunteers served in CD, but this soon was terminated because the German and Dutch youth had considerably different interests, including shorter work terms. Language differences also played a role. When a Dutch participant asked why they could not cooperate with the Germans, the CD director replied, "Why don't you start a program of your own? It will help by giving advice and ideas."[207] Apparently the cultural and theological perspectives were sufficiently different to preclude working together.

Young people in France and Switzerland were shifted to respective church projects including Bible and service camps.[208] But the French did not continue the voluntary service program as such. The theological orientation of the latter two Mennonite conferences, which were supporters of MVS during the post-World War II emergencies, apparently was not able to integrate the concept of ProSocial service into their understandings of biblical Christianity and the Anabaptist/believers church view of mutual aid and service when the "world" returned to normal. Soon after the German CD was formed, a project was conducted in France, and the French young people were invited to participate. But the French question was, "Is it social or is it Christian? I told them for me they are not different; they are together, service is mission."[209]

This dramatic tension and ultimately parting of the ways of MVS in Europe reflects a subplot of broader movement and theology called the "Fundamentalist-Evangelical" movement. This influence was opposed by the Anabaptist theology which sees the gospel as a unified effort of other-worldly salvation and this-worldly justice and righteousness. Undoubtedly it was this major underlying factor that created the tension in the emergence, operation, and demise of MVS. This tension tended to divide the France and Swiss churches from the Dutch and the German for considerable decades, the former being the more evangelical and pietistic. This helps to explain why the Germans and the Dutch continued with the formation of national voluntary service programs of their own.[210]

The issue which became critical in the dissolution of MVS was differing positions on the connection between witness and service among the sponsoring conferences. Was witness to the Christian gospel basically proclamation? Was service basically not witnessing? Or could they be one and the same? Voluntary service is probably one of the most direct and specific expressions of a union of witness and service. It is literally responding directly to the total person's need. In fact, I propose that "one may witness to others by words alone, but one cannot serve others without at the same witnessing to one's faith. The latter does both while the former does only one."[211]

Surry, England, MVS work camp, 1968. Courtesy Jaap Rem

MVS Council, 1958, left to right: Richard Hertzler, Germany; Howard Birky (Paxman); Anneliese Dyck (MVS secretary); Leenie de Groot, Netherlands; Erika Nussbaumer, Switzerland; Erwin Goering, MVS director; Jean Jacques Hirschey, France; Hans-Jacob Galle, Germany. Courtesy Howard Birkey

Above and left: Stages in the Witmarsum Church, joint Pax and MVS project, 1960. Courtesy Loyal Klassen

Chapter 6

THE CONTEXT AND THE VISION

W hat has been the substance of the MVS experience? Are
there generalizations that can be made? The following
seem appropriate:

A. The Substance

- The objective of providing social, psychological, and spiritual sustenance to young people, especially in Europe but wherever camps were established, was generally achieved, although there were mistakes and failures. The building of friendships, the creation of trust and acceptance across various barriers and boundaries was palpable. Though a specific religious witness dimension was not aggressively presented and promoted, reconciliation and spiritual understanding via service rather than preaching was nevertheless everywhere experienced daily.[212]
- The objectives of meeting emergency physical and material needs were primarily achieved, although in limited and modest fashion—meaning there were few major projects that were fully completed, as for example the construction of a youth center, or a home. (There were several exceptions, such as the church at Witmarsum, the Netherlands—a combined Pax-MVS effort.)
- Introducing and encouraging people to do voluntary service by way of the work camp movement was effective for

many camp participants. The concept of voluntary service was new and made lasting impact on many if not most campers. Serving others voluntarily, without coercion or reward, seemed to be a new idea which was eagerly embraced. It was this Anabaptist value even more than pacifism that mystified many, but it convinced many if not most participants and may have had a lasting impact on their lives.

• The setting of MVS, including the social, political, and economic context of the MVS program, changed rather rapidly. By the mid-1950s, Europe was on the road to recovery and the emergency character of the needs had began to decrease; this was so especially in Germany which because of the Marshal Plan witnessed the "miracle" of post-World War II European recovery. (Note the profile of voluntary service globally in Table 5). Can a service program weather rapid underlying social changes?

• As the emergency social and economic crises resulting from World War II were being solved, the need for refugee housing, youth and recreational facilities, etc. could now be met by the locality or the countries in question. Could service have other forms? What did this say about external factors and service?

• The types of camps show the gradual decrease in emergency projects in Germany, as the focus shifted to countries with less direct World War II destruction and emphasized more community development. This reflects the significance of the context, discussed above.

• In the context of this reduced emergency, young people were beginning to feel the pull of moving into personal careers and other possibilities, and opportunities to do so began to flourish. The camp volunteers thus began to show more interest in more international experiences, while the number of urgent projects also diminished.

• The role and need of work camps to provide an opportunity for young people to build friendships, find meaningful work, and even room and board for a summer away from school was no longer as urgent and was replaced by the new social and cultural institutions. Travel and vacations in other countries often stirred hunger for new relationships.

- The socio-political developments of the late 1960s and early 1970s began to create a gap between the "Establishment" generation and the "Sixties" youth. Thus the most recent volunteers were much less idealistic about their contribution and more cynical about what could be done in the face of selfish and vested interests than the 1950s volunteers had been.
- The urgency of World War II trauma and the great stresses of postwar reconstruction had helped bridge the differences between the Mennonite Conferences in France, Germany, Switzerland, and the Netherlands. But with recovery, the work camp movement, which had become established as a central youth program for the European conferences, also began to be looked at a bit more critically. And as noted above, differing perceptions of the appropriateness of the MVS for the European Mennonites began to emerge.
- MCC's slow but steady withdrawal from involvement in European Mennonite affairs was another factor in the demise of MVS. The European Mennonites were regaining religious, economic, and social stability and depended less and less on the Americans. The formation of the European relief organization (IMO) by the Dutch and German Mennonites is an illustration of this change. As is indicated below, the French and Swiss Mennonites caution of "social service" actions were not ready to participate in the more "socially" oriented IMO.[213]
- For the European MVS program, a more fundamental dissonance began to surface in the Mennonite supporting constituency between those national groups which were concerned about responding to the social and economic as well as spiritual needs they felt were a part of the Christian faith—as against those afraid of the secularization influences of "social action" and how it might negatively affect witnessing to the faith and spiritual life of the young people and the recipients.
- Adminstration of the European MVS camp program was fairly uniform from the beginning, even though there had been an "adaptive evolution" in form and structure as European young people began to take on leadership of MVS.

Although there may be other factors, these conclusions at least point to the many factors causing the demise of MVS and beg deeper analysis.[214]

Nevertheless, the MVS European story, seen from the perspective of the volunteers and the Mennonite community, was significant and indelible. Richard Hertzler, who clearly understood the vision of MVS and was one of the most indefatigable supporters from the beginnings of MVS until he died, expressed the vision as follows:

> The significance of MFD for the Mennonite brotherhood lies first of all in the fellowship of Mennonite youth from various countries, then further the opportunity for contact with Christian youth from other countries and circumstances, but also in the privilege of putting into practice the command of Christ to love one's neighbor as himself, and to give an example to others of this spirit.[215]

B. The Story Line

What is the story line of the MVS saga? What has been the meaning and contribution, if any, of MVS to the Mennonite, Christian, and even the larger human story? It has been often said that the human story is a struggle of good and evil "or the other way around." In a review of the film "The Rape of Nanking," which recounts the awful murder, rape, and burning of Nanking by the Japanese, Stephen Hunter asks, "What does Nanking prove?" He answers his own question: "Man is evil, but men can be good. Or, men are evil, but man can be good. I don't know." He concludes by asking, So what do we learn from history?[216]

We have learned from the human saga that every act, whether good or evil, requires a context—a social and cultural environment in which these two forces are played out. In fact, it is only in the context of the situation that human propensities are brought to fruition and receive their meaning. I propose that MVS was a phenomenon that took place in a unique context. Yet it was also archetypal by definition. Young people acted in a specific context and were motivated by those particular contextual forces, yet their response was one of compassion. MVS represented humans doing good, undoing what other humans (doing evil?) had done. But it was also loving service expressed "in the Name of Christ" which raised it to Christian service.

This is not the place to launch an analysis of human motivations, actions, and consequences. It has been done copiously elsewhere. But it is possible to present a simple proposition which has profound implications in regard to the good-and-evil philosophy outlined above. It is the counter-proposition to evil, no, rather, a universal axiom: "Love your neighbor as yourself." Stated another way, "Do unto others as you would have them do unto you."[217] This double axiom proclaimed by Jesus simply states that loving others is how we can really love ourselves as well.[218] Jesus himself demonstrated this principle by giving his life for others. "Among you, whoever wants to be great must be your servant, and whoever wants to be first must be the willing servant of all. For even the Son of man did not come to be served, but to serve, and to surrender his life as a ransom for many" (Mark 10:42-45).

The MVS story is based on love as the core basis for human survival that flies headlong into the face of history. "Philosophers going back to Plato and Aristotle have argued that people are fundamentally driven by self-love and self-interest. . . ." We tend to love ourselves rather than others, hence "the assumption of universal egoism is so fundamental and widespread in our culture that it is hard to recognize, like water for a fish."[219]

The spirit of love was expressed by Jesus in the almost universally familiar Good Samaritan story. The lawyer wanted to know what the fundamental law of life was. Jesus asked him the famous question, Who was the good neighbor to the victim of robbery?" The lawyer was no dummy, and replied, "The one who showed him kindness." And Jesus said, "Go and do as he did (Luke 10:36-37). Voluntarily serving others, (doing good) or "loving your neighbor as yourself " is one of the greatest stories ever told. The MVS saga is one little chapter in the ever continuing expression of the greatest commandment—love.

Within this framework and foundation, some concluding vignettes are presented to describe the atmosphere and spirit which prevailed throughout the MVS program from beginning to its termination and its contribution to the larger goal of "doing good."[220] The following unsolicited reflections, among many others, were sent in by a group of English volunteers to the MVS Newsletter editor.[221] The letter informs us of the type of work they campers performed, their relationships in the camps and the community, and the meanings they derived from the work:

> Now as the winter months draw in and we are set-
> tling down once more to office routine our thoughts
> stray back to the six months which will always remain
> imprinted in our minds, this is the period of time that
> we spent with MVS in Europe. The majority of our time
> was spent in MVS work camps in France, Austria, and
> Germany, while the rest was in children's homes and
> farming. As you can imagine, there was a tremendous
> variety in the tasks we undertook, and they were very
> different to the jobs we had been doing in England, but
> despite this difference we *reveled in the work and we had a*
> *glorious time.*[222]
>
> The most wonderful memories we have are of the
> people we met and the kindness and hospitality they
> showed toward us wherever we went. Not only from
> the campers themselves did we get this wonderful feel-
> ing of friendliness, but we were helped considerably by
> complete strangers such as Railway Staff and local
> Shopkeepers. Looking back now all pains and blisters
> are forgotten and we remember only the exhilarating
> feelings of freedom, fellowship ands spiritual under-
> standing that was reached between everyone we en-
> countered so breaking down barriers created by differ-
> ent nationalities and religious.
>
> Although we had to say goodbye to many newly
> made friends this thought remains: THAT WE MAY
> STILL BE JOINED IN HEART AND HOPE TO MEET
> AGAIN. (You may be interested to know the three
> campers, Mavies Summersby, Joyce Blunson and
> Brenda Walters, hold the record of continuous uninter-
> rupted service with MVS this year. They joined the

Guebwiller/France Easter camp, then served in the children's home until the Annabereg/Austria camp opened. They served in Annaberg from start to finish. Next they worked on a German vegetable and fruit farm. Next to West Berlin; after the close of that camp, they went to Grefrath. Here they helped finish the camp and stayed on for about two additional weeks and worked. Service? A "mind to work"?) Our sincere thanks for MVS's fine work.[223]

The effects of MVS on the participants was vast, and many persons maintain that it was the "turning point" of their lives. A personal integration of identity and purpose for life and career was almost always a central function of voluntary service. For most participants an opportunity to express their faith by helping others was dominant, and when this fundamental basis seemed to shift, the voluntary service program had to change. In addition, the families and communities that received help from MVS camp projects still remember with gratitude the contributions the young people made to them, and many lasting friendships were established. A great service was given.

The European MVS story suggests that the voluntary service idea was idealistic and religious. The motive for the activity was basically a religious ethic—serving (and witnessing to) others. The following testimony by a camper, one of hundreds in the files of MVS, provides a fitting conclusion.

An international work camp is like a cool breath of air: it refreshes the spirit and opens the eyes. An international work camp is an experience that lives on in our memories rising above the mundane things that usually crowd our minds. It is a mountain top experience that ingrains itself so deeply in our character that it can effect the most antagonistic personality despite himself. To the Christian it is an experience in living as the early saints lived. For what do we have in a work camp but people of all different backgrounds joined together to do a work of love, without pay, their closest bond— Christian love.[224]

Abover: Enkenbach, Germany, MVS work camp, preparing site for the Mennonite church, 1956. Below: Enkenbach, 1956. Fir Enkenbach MVS group from England, Germany, Holland, and the U.S. Courtesy Loyal Klassen

An enthusiastic group of over 60 MVSers gathering for a conference, November 1956. Courtesy Loyal Klassen

Warga, Netherlands, 1960 reunion of former Warga MVS work campers. Courtesy Loyal Klassen.

Table 1. Tabulation of International Work Camps

YEAR	# OF CAMPS	COUNTRIES IN WHICH CAMPS WERE CONDUCTED							
1948	2	Germ. 2							
1949	3	Germ. 2	Holl. 1						
1950	7	Germ. 5	France 1	Italy 1					
1951	6	Germ. 4	Switz. 1	Belgium 1					
1952	11	Germ. 8	Austria 1	Italy 1	Luxem. 1				
1953	7	Germ. 2	Austria 1	Holl. 3	France 1				
1954	6	Austria	Holl.	Germ. ???					
1955	6	Germ. 2	Holl. 2	Austria 1	Greece 1				
1956	7	Germ. 4	France 3						
1957	16	Holl. 4	Germ. 3	France 3	Austria 3				
1958	16	Germ. 6	Nether. 4	France 3	Austria 3				
1959	10	Germ. 4	Austria 4	France 21	Greece 1				
1960	16	Germ. 6	Austria 5	France 3	Nether. 2				
1961	15	Germ. 4	Austria 3	France 3	Greece 2	Italy 1	Algeria 1		
1962	20	Germ. 5	Austria 4	Nether. 4	France 3	Algeria 1 Great Br. 1			
1963	14	Germ. 4	France 3	Belgium 2	Greece 1	Nether. 1	Switz. 1	Austria 1	Great Br. 1
1964	16	Germ. 5	France 4	Greece 2	Austria 2	Nether. 1	Morocco 1		
1965	12	Germ. 5	France 4	Austria 2	Greece 1				
1966	14	Germ. 6	Greece 2	France 1	Belgium 1	Great Br. 1	Austria 1	Israel 1	Switz. 1
1967	13	Germ. 5	France 2	Israel 1	Switz. 1	Yugos. 1	Great Br. 1	Austria 1	Greece 1
1968	13	Austria 1	England1	Germ.6	Greece1	France 1	Nether. 1	Israel 1	Yugos. 1
1969	17	Germ. 5	France 3	Greece 2	Israel 1	Luxem. 1	Switz. 1	Austria1	Austria1
1970	15	Germ. 4	France 3	Greece 2	Great Br. 2	Israel 1	Switz. 1	Austria 1	Nether. 1

Table 1 Sources: MVS *Newsletters,* Annual Reports, MVS office; Ortwin Driedger, "MVS-1948-1971" (Feb. 2004), Wierhof archives, whose summary omits 1959-1961. At least 262 camps, including Easter camps, operated 1948-1970. This figure is not fully accurate, since information for several years is not complete The height was reached in 1962, with 20 camps. Germany received the most help with 96 followed by France and Austria, tied at 35 eachm, then the Netherlands 24, Greece 14, Great Britain 9, Switzerland 7, Israel and Belgium 4 each. Algeria, Morocco, Spain, Luxemburg, and Yugoslavia had 1 each. The total and the number for each country do not add up since there were repeat camps in several countries as noted.

Table 2. MVS VOLUNTEERS
FROM FOLLOWING COUNTRIES

EUROPE	1957	1958	1959	1960
Holland	93	65	100	87 [225]
Germany	41	50	51	74
England	37	46	14	30
Sweden	11	17	24	37
Greece	6	19	14	10
Denmark	3	9	20	14
France	5	9	3	3
Switzerland	5	7	2	
Italy	4	3	3	2
Norway	4	3	1	2
Spain	8	2	5	3
Finland	3	1	1	
Portugal	3			
Yugos.	3			
Poland	2			
Austria	9	3	2	
Hungary	1	2		
Luxemburg	3			
AFRICA				
Egypt	4	5	1	1
Ethopia/				
Ghana	1			
ASIA				
Turkey	4	3	3	1
Lebanon	1			
India	22			
N. AMERICA				
U.S.	37	47	37	41
Canada	7	4	1	4

Table 2 source: MVS *Newsletter;* Ortwin Driedger, op. cit.

Table 3. NUMBER OF WORK CAMPS AND PARTICIPANTS
(*arranged by continent and country by 1955*)

COUNTRY	CAMPS	PARTICIPANTS
AFRICA		
Algeria-France	9	144
Egypt	2	1121
French Camer-	1	42
oons (Fr)		
N. Rhodesia (UK)	1	350
Tunisia (Fr)	1	14
Union of South	2	55
Africa		
Subtotal	*16*	*1732*
AMERICAS		
Alaska (sic)	4	26
Brazil	1	31
Canada	1	20
Cuba	1	16
Salvador	1	13
Jamaica (UK)	1	12
Mexico	12	237
Puerto Rico (US)	6	90
United States	613	6419
Subtotal	*640*	*6864*
AUSTRALASIA		
Cyprus (UK)	2	29
Hong Kong (UIC)	1	30
New Zealand	140	
Subtotal	*487*	*35706*
EUROPE		
Austria	49	1,305
Belgium	7	416
Denmark	7	96
Finland	9	171
France	107	2403
Germany	57	5593
Greece	6	129
Italy	10	575
Netherlands	14	732
Norway	6	168
Spain	77	1,983
Sweden	38	684
Switzerland	5	152
United Kingdom	118	5562
Yugoslavia	6	5012
Subtotal	*716*	*24981*
GRAND TOTAL	**1,859**	**69283**

Table 3 source: CCIVWC–UNESCO released to *MVS Newsletter*, June 1955.

Appendix 1

ACCOUNT OF ORGANIZATIONAL MEETING OF MENNONITE VOLUNTARY SERVICE

Temporary Meeting of Mennonite Voluntary Service (*Mennonitischen Freiwillingendienstes*)

I.

a) At the invitation of MCCC in fall 1950, the Mennonites of Germany, France, Netherlands and Switzerland each nominated a representative for the creation of an organization, which should take over the Voluntary service program in Europe, which MCC had begun. On the basis of discussion, it was decided to ask MCC to become a fifth member of the organization, and at least for the time being to continue administration of the program, at Frankfurt/Main. The organization was given the name Mennonitischer Freiwilligendienst (MFD)—Mennonite Voluntary Service.

b). Since the form and structure of this project (Arbeit) for the future is not yet clear, the definite "constitution" could not be stated at the first meeting.. At the second meeting of this committee, the following "constitution" was temporarily proposed and accepted.

II.

a) the present statutes are therefore valid, until the permanent statutes replace them.

b) Until the permanent constitution and by laws are formulated, MCC will function as the legal entity in so far as the representatives, at the present time, are not able to derive their legal standing from the sponsoring Mennonite conferences in each country.

c). The goal of this organization is the creation and implementing the Mennonite voluntary Service program in Europe. Thereby shall:

1. A Christian service for the benefit of those in need shall be carried out.

2. The Mennonite church's young peoples shall be given the opportunity to voluntarily serve as representatives of the Mennonite Congregations and Conferences.

d) A Christian witness shall be given through the work, through contact with the camp participants, including the non-Mennonites, and contact with the people in the recipient community.

e) The Concrete Responsibilities shall be:

1) for the representatives from the national Mennonite conferences :

a) To be the spokespersons/promoters for the MFD (MVS) in their respective lands, and to encourage participation by young people in the program.

b) To promote active and energetic contact with the youth groups of their respective countries.

c) To with the involvement of the various national youth organizations to locate promising projects and carry them, in close coordination with the secretariat of MFD.

2) for the executive office:

a) To carry out the business and operational affairs of the organization.

b) To make and maintain contacts with other organizations in other countries and camp participants in countries where Mennonite and non-Mennonite.

c) To locate work projects and operate them in various countries, insofar as they are no processed by the MFD representatives.

d) To compile and disseminate information from all the activities of MFD to all the participant campers to keep and strengthen relationships among them strong.

This provisional constitution was recorded at the meeting of the executive council on April 10 1951 and Espelkamp, Westfahlen.

Present were: Samuel Gerber, Switzerland; Ernst Hege, France; Richard Hertzler, Germany; Paul Peachey, MCC (Frankfurt); Cal Redekop, MCC (Frankfurt). Note: No Dutch representative was present at these first meetings, though the Dutch Mennonite Church later became very supportive and active in the program. *Source: Original typescript in author's MVS files.*

VOLUNTARY SERVICE RESPONSES IN POST-WORLD WAR II EUROPE: A TIMELINE

I. Major International Actions

1. 1946. UNRRA (United Nations Relief and Rehabilitation Association)

2. 1946. UNESCO (United Nations Education. Scientific and Cultural Organization)

3. 1946. CRALOG (Council of Relief Organizations for Operation in Germany), eleven organizations, including Brethren Service Commission and MCC.

4. 1948. ECA (European Recovery Plan, i.e. "Marshal Plan"). Ended in 1951 succeeded by Organization for Economic Cooperation which included European nations).

II. International Voluntary Service Developments

1. 1950. CCIWC (UNESCO-sponsored Coordination Council for International Work Camps). Paris.

2. 1950. AIWCG (Association of International Work Camps in Germany.

III. Mennonite and Related Group Post-World War II ServiceActivities

1. MCC and MRC reconstruction builders units, 1947

1. 1948. Council of Mennonite Colleges "Study/work terms" in

Germany.

2. 1949. First International Work Camps sponsored by MCC and Church of the Brethren.

3. 1950. MVS (Mennonite Voluntary Service) sponsored by Dutch, French, German, Swiss, and MCC).

4. 1951. Pax (MCC alternative service program for COs). BSC initiated similar program and cooperated with Pax.

5. 1953. IVS (International Voluntary Service), sponsored by Brethren, Mennonites and Friends to provided alternative service for COs financed by the U.S. government through USAID.

6. 1957. EIRENE (International Christian Service for Peace), sponsored by Mennonites, Brethren, International Fellowship of Reconciliation) as alternative for military service for COs.

7. 1961. PEACE CORPS, U.S. government-sponsored voluntary service organization, indirectly influenced by Peace Church service organizations.

NOTES

Abbreviation: *ME: Mennonite Encyclopedia* vols. 1-5 (Scottdale, Pa.: Herald Press, vols. 1-4, 1955, 1956, 1957, 1959; vol. 5, 1990).

1. There are archetypal experiences and relationships most everyone is privileged to have, and not restricted to work camps. But I also believe the atmosphere and spirit of voluntary service projects and camps are of unusual vitality, meaning, and satisfaction. They cannot be totally duplicated and must be experienced to be understood.

2. Cereso's work is described briefly in chapter 1.

3. Donald F. Durnbaugh, "Mutual Aid and Service," *The Believers' Church* (Scottdale, Pa.: Herald Press, 1968), 277.

4. The Church of the Brethren, Quakers, and Mennonites

5. However European voluntary service organizations began to emerge during this time as well but they cannot be described here.

6. The many directories indicate that there are literally thousands of organizations located in many countries that promote voluntary service in almost every nation on earth.

7. Dolly Daftary and Amanda Moore McBride, "International Voluntary Service," http://atlas-conferences.com/c/a/m/k/87.htm

8. The emotional and psychological destruction suffered by the people was much more serious, but this became evident to me especially as I began my work with German refugee.

9. There apparently is no action in Europe or America to document this story.

10. Paraphrased from *Vive sa veritee*, meaning the Prince of Peace (Baconneiere, Neuchatel, Switzerland, 1950).

11. There are surely instances of other voluntary service activities.

12. See Albert Keim, *The CPS Story* (Intercourse, Pa.: Good Books, 1990).

13. Melvin Gingerich, "Civilian Public Service," *ME* 1, 611.

14. John D. Unruh, *In the Name of Christ* (Scottdale, Pa.: Herald Press, 1952), 266.

15. The work the CPS program was of course determined by Selective Service restrictions.

16. John D. Unruh, *In the Name of Christ*, 266.

17. Wilfred Unruh, *A Study of Mennonite Service Programs* (AMBS:

Elkhart, Ind., 1965), 85.

18. John D. Unruh, 295. For the best brief survey of voluntary service developments in the United States, see H. S. Bender, "Voluntary Service," *ME* 4, 848-850.

19. "Our Colleges and the Voluntary Service Program in the Present Crisis," *Proceedings of the Conferences on Mennonite Educational and Cultural Problems* 8 (1951), 55.

20. *MCC Annual Meeting,* Dec.-Jan. 1, 1945-46, 6. These camps resulted mainly from the desire of women to serve in a fashion equivalent to that of the men inducted into CPS.

21. Before this period the great technical hindrances in communication contributed to the separate directions the European and American Mennonites took. See "Mennonite World Conference," *ME* 3, 640-642.

22. The first picture in this book, taken in early 1950 from the Frankfurt Dom, shows the destruction of central Frankfurt, Germany. The pictures in this book not attributed are furnished by the author.

23. Irvin B Horst, *A Ministry of Goodwill* (Akron, Pa.: Mennonite Central Committee, 1950), 65. See also John D. Unruh, *In the Name of Christ*, 147-164.

24. Ibid., 65-67.

25. Ibid., 66-67.

26. John D. Unruh, *In the Name of Christ.* See chapter 16, "Voluntary Service," for a brief history of voluntary service in North America and in Europe.

27. "Council of Mennonite and Affiliated Colleges," *ME* 1, 722.

28. John D. Unruh, 300.

29. Ibid., 301; See also "Council of Mennonite and Affiliated Colleges," ME 1, 722-723.

30. *Der Mennonit,* March/April, 1948, 25. "In addition to the 45 Americans, 40 to 50 selected German youth will also participate," 25.

31. See *Voluntary Service Report,* 1948ff (MCC, mimeo).

32. *Voluntary Service Letter,* March 1949. See also W. Unruh, A-184.

33. Emily Brunk, *Espelkamp* (Karlsruhe, Germany: MCC/Henrich Schnieder,1951), 23.

34. Milton Harder lived several miles up the road from my home near Butterfield, Minn., and his decisions influenced my decision to join MCC.

35. Brunk, op. cit.

36. Milton Harder, "'Die Mennoniten' at Espelkamp," *Mennonite Life* (July 1952): 109.

37. Ibid., 109. For a brief survey of the early European Mennonite Voluntary Service program until 1965, see Wilfred Unruh, *A Study of Mennonite Service Programs.* A-183-199.

38. Paul Peachey, "Voluntary Service Report," Summer Program (MCC, mimeo), 1949, 3.

39. The financial costs of the camps were carried by MCC cash subsidies, supplies of relief food, contributions from the local business and governments. Each camp had its own configuration of the above.

40. Paul Peachey, *Voluntary Service Report*, 1949, 10.

41. This story will not fully describe the context of the post-WWII situation in Germany or Europe, since it is generally widely known.

42. Harder, "'Die Mennoniten' at Espelkamp," *Mennonite Life* (July 1952): 109.
Of the ninety volunteers, eighty were Mennonite, thirteen Protestants, one Catholic, and one Church of England.

43. The Espelkamp of today would not be recognized by some who visited there in the 1950s.

44. I arrived at Espelkamp, Germany, on January 28, 1950, and spent the first three months there. It was a cold, primitive, and austere introduction In April 1950 I received a note from Paul Peachey in Frankfurt asking me to come at the first opportunity to discuss my helping administer the growing work camp program. I did not tell my fellows VSers how happy I was to get away from the dreary area and go to the "big city." However, spending some time at Espelkamp was very important. Because I had noted many of the problems and challenges of conducting a long-term work camp, as the MVS program grew and the Pax program was initiated, I was helped in anticipating many pitfalls and challenges

45. Espelkamp was in a deep forest, hidden far from other German villages. The army barrack got so cold at night ice formed on our faces. Sleeping dormitory style in bunks two tiers high, we hit the cold floor in the dark, and in an instant tiptoed to the small room with several basins where we brushed teeth and washed. We quickly donned clothes to be presentable and raced to the combination living, dining, and kitchen areas, where a roaring fire was already making a cozy room, inviting us to help with getting breakfast ready. The dread I felt of getting out on the cold project by 8:30, new snow on the ground, wind blowing, and no sun was huge, but I determined that if Milton could take it, so could I.

46. Emily Brunk, *Espelkamp*. For a personal account of the first year of the camp, see William O. Dick, *Espelkamp on the German Frontier* (Austin ,Tex.:, privately published by Ruth Anne Abraham, 2005).

47. An interesting byproduct of this unit was the involvement of the Conservative Amish Mennonite Conference. From the beginning of the camp, personnel from the Conservative conference had participated and slowly begun to develop very significant relationships with the local population by way of Bible studies and other religious and educational and social services. In 1950 the Conservative Amish Mennonite mission board appointed its first representative (Johnny and Grace Gingerich) and later took over the operation of the voluntary service unit which has continued very effectively to serve the many thousands of refuges from the east. Most of the personnel were volunteers who served two or more years. The Gingerichs established such an important relationship with people in the developing city of Espelkamp that a street subsequently was named after them—Johnny Gingerich Strasse.

48. *MCC Annual Meeting Minutes*, Jan. 1, 1949, 4.

49. "In March, 10, 1950, the new home was finally dedicated. At this time MCC expressed its pleasure to cooperate with various voluntary service organizations working in Germany." *Der Mennonit*, July 1950, 54.

50. Paul Peachey, *Voluntary Service Report: Summer Programs 1949*, MCC, 10.

51. *Der Mennonit*, Nov. 1950, 118. Another example: An applicant for a spot in a work camp in 1950 was rejected because he did not meet the requirements. His father thereupon made a costly trip to the VS headquarters to plead for his son. The father stated that the son had been thoroughly emotionally damaged by the war experiences and literally begged that he be given a chance. The VS office conditionally accepted him. The father, in letter a year later stated that he believed it had been the work camp experience that had given his son a hope and direction in life. To underline his thankfulness, the father, a noted artist, donated several paintings to the VS office.

52. Certainly from 1948 to 1952, when I left Europe, many were motivated to come to the camps because they were given good nourishing food, which they had not had for a long time.

53. Letter from Wienss, Nov. 2, 2006. John D. Unruh says "It seems that the voluntary work camps touched Europe's youth in a more challenging way then the large-scale material aid distribution programs (conducted by MCC)," 303.

54. For example, at the Ronneburg "Campers Reunion," Guy F. Hershberger had led a discussion on American peace witness and activities. Peachey, *Voluntary Service*, 10.

55. As result of this growth, as indicated above, I was transferred to the MCC office in April to help in the planning and directing of the voluntary service program including the Espelkamp project.

56. *MCC Voluntary Service Letter* 12, May 1950. See Appendixes for details regarding details of volunteers. See also Calvin Redekop, "European Mennonite Voluntary Service," *Mennonite Life* (July 1952): 106-108 for brief history of MVS and listing of camps from 1950-1952.

57. I consulted often with MVS board members for advice.

58. April 1950. The camp was conducted during July-August 1950.

59. If rejected, it required writing a "Dear John letter," which was never pleasant.

60. Where I became addicted to the German *Wuerstchin*, or Bockwurst.

61. Calvin Redekop, "Development of Voluntary Service in Europe," *Gospel Herald*, January 1952, 88.

62. *MCC Activity Report*, July 1951.

63. General Lewis Hershey, director of Selective Service, was most impressed with the Mainz camp and the peace significance.

64. Letter to John Howard Yoder, director of the French MCC program, Sept. 1950.

65. MFD—*Mennonitischen Freiwilligen Dienst*. These men came since

they had already indicated their deep interest in supporting the VS idea.

66. They were John Fox, Mel Hedrick, and Paul Suderman. *MCC Voluntary Service Letter*, Oct. 1950.

67. As with the PAX program, the German government assisted with the costs of constructing housing, but a down payment of "self help" was required from the refugees, and the VS team helped to initiate this action.

68. MCC *Voluntary Service Letter* 15, Oct./Nov. 1950.

69. Edited from monthly report.

70. Considerable information for th first days of Caravan was provided in correspondence of Bob Lee and his *MVS Annual Report*, Nov.-1951-Sept. 1952. See an excellent report, including pictures, by Richard Rush in *MVS Caravan, From my Personal Diary 1952* (n.d.). See also *Zeilsheim/FFM Work Camp, Jan 2-Feb 25, 1952*—a twenty-four-page journal of the camp, which lists the names of fourteen volunteers who served at the camp. Richard Rush's report contains a vivid comparison of the church building under construction and a recent photo taken in 1980 in which it is in full use.

71. Richard Rush, *From My Personal Diary*, 5; Bob Lee, 17.

72. Bob Lee, *Annual Report*, 4-5.

73. Ibid., 6. See also Richard Rush, 6. Rush's account provides interesting and pictorial accounts of early MVS Caravan activities.

74. *MVS Newsletter*, June 1952, 2.

75. These persons were Curt Janzen, Bob Lee, Sol Yoder, and Hugo Friesen.

76. Bob Lee, 9.

77. The memory of Ceresole's vision of international voluntary service for conscientious objectors was still alive among the work campers and many citizens at large. This concern developed into the Pax program, referred to below. In the summer of 1950, the Frankfurt voluntary service office became concerned about the possibility of protracted of conflict in Korea and wondered whether the European work-camp program might become an alternative service option for conscientious objectors. *Voluntary Service Letter*, May 1950.

78. *Voluntary Service Letter*, April 1949.

79. *CCIVWC Reports*, c/o Youth Section UNESCO, 1953. Hans-Joachim Wienss states that the organization was "later simply called COCO." He states that "there [developed] a political line dividing the representatives from the two sides of the 'Iron Curtain.'" Personal correspondence, Nov. 2, 2006.

80. By 1954, the CCIVWC reported that 69,283 young people participated in 1,859 work camps around the globe. An example was the work in India, where roads, wells, sanitation, and irrigation projects were completed. *MVS Newsletter*, April 1955, 4-5; Calvin W. Redekop, *The Pax Story* (Telford, Pa.: Pandora Press U.S., 2001), 76.

81. *MVS Newsletter*, April 1952, 3

82. "As you know, MVS, receives its grant of money from the Bonn

Government through the AIG." LaMarr Kopp, *Report to the MVS Council,* April 30, 1955, 1.

83. Report submitted March 1, 1955, to AIG.

84. The Church of the Brethren was actively involved in the voluntary service movement. See J. Kenneth Kreider, *A Cup of Cold Water: The Story of Brethren Service* (Elgin, Ill.: Brethren Press, 2001). The COB was involved in an amazingly wide variety of camps and programs, and were more ecumenical, cooperating with Lutheran World Service and the World Council of Churches, the latter on a major development project in Greece. See Kreider, chapter 12, "Brethren Service in Greece and Turkey," 265-286.

85. M.V.S (sic). Camp Leaders' Conference Report, Frankfurt, June 16, 1952.

86. As for example the Dutch V.S. Conference, held on June 2-3, 1951, at Heerwegen Holland. The experiences of Dutch Mennonite campers were presented, and discussion proceeded regarding the significance of the MVS idea, including the opportunities of ecumenical relationship and international reconciliation, especially between the Dutch and Germans.

87. Ibid., 5. For a general description of the expectations, see also Wilfred Unruh, A-187ff.

88. *Minutes,* MVS Council, Basel, February 16, 1952.

89. Gerhard Hildebrand, Calvin Redekop and Theo Glueck, *Die Jugend auf der Weltkonferenz,* mimeo, Aug. 1952, 4.

90. *Mennonitische Jugend: Nachrichten aus der Jugendarbeit,* mimeo, Oct. 1952, 2.

91. The reporting on the MVS program an the sources from this date on are based on secondary sources and other MVS participants.

92. *MVS Newsletter,* April 1953, 2.

93. Ibid., September 3. Der Vries also states that a number of Pax men had participated in the camps. It included a letter from a Pax man stating, "I enjoyed my working in MVS and I can truthfully say it has been the best year of my life," 3.

94. *MVS Newsletter,* Nov. 1954, 3.

95. Resource material exists in the MCC files at Akron, Pa., Mennonite Church archives; at Goshen, Ind.; and at Mennonitischen Forshgungs Stelle at Weirhof, Pfalz, Germany, among other places.

96. *MVS Newsletter* April 1955, 1. FAU refers to Friends Ambulance Unit.

97. LaMarr Kopp letter to MVS council, November 5, 1954. Some confusion emerged regarding this action, since the Dutch Mennonites thought that MVS was aiming to become a camp for "pacifists only." This misunderstanding was cleared up in early 1955, when Kopp assured the Dutch that MVS was open to people from all political and religious persuasions. Report to the MVS council, March 1955.

98. Ibid., October 1955, 3-9

99. It seems the German Red Cross and other organizations were becoming aware of the contribution that MVS was making, especially

in Germany, *MVS Newsletter*, April 1955, 5.

100. For an account of the Karlsschule Project, see Merlin Garber (*Karlsschule*, n.p. 1983). See also Kreider, *A Cup of Cold Water*, 198-203.

101. *MVS Newsletter*, October 1955, 9. This MVS project played a large role in the subsequent Pax and the Brethren Service Commission programs. The BSC volunteers had begun the project, which became a joint BSC-PAX project. MVS was involve both with the Caravan and a work camp. See Calvin Redekop, *The Pax Story*, 65-66, for an account of the Pax involvements.

102. Space prohibits descriptions of each camp. However, the *MVS Newsletters*, which contain the more detailed descriptions of the camps, are available in the archives of the Mennonite Church, Goshen, Ind., as well as the Eastern Mennonite University Mennonite Historical Library.

103. *MVS Newsletter*, March 1957.

104. *MVS Newsletter*, March 1957, 6.

105. Ibid., 7. At least two dozen Easter work camps were mounted

106. See for example, *Het Algemeen Handelsblad*, June 1956. "A very enthusiastic reunion was staged at the Warga church on September 19, 2003. A total of 13 campers, many with spouses, attended the celebration."

107. *MVS Newsletter*, October 1959. Some of the camps lasted up to two weeks.

108. *MVS Newsletter*, Feb. 1960.

109. MVS *Newsletter*, Jan. 1961

110. See photo. See also *Mennonite Life* (Jan. 1961) for additional photos.

111. For example, the construction of a school in Agadir took place in cooperation with EIRENE, described above. This project involved more community development work, which Eirene and Pax were pioneering in Greece and Morocco.

112. See for example *Pax Newsletter*, October 1955: "PAX-MVS boys [sic] have been traveling to all directions recently."

113. Richard Hertzler, "Mennonitscher Freiwilligendienst," *ME* 3:649. In 1967 the office was moved to Eysseneckstrassse 54, Frankfurt/Main, close to Vogtstrasse 44 where it began.

114. The terms did not conform to calendar years in numerous cases.

115. This figure does not total Driedger's tally since he did not include Easter camps and does not have figures for 1959-1961.

116. See the tables of work camps. The total and the number for each country do not add up to the same number since there were some repeat camps in several countries

117. Don Luce, "Introduction," in *The IVS Experience from Algeria to Vietnam*, ed. Stuart Rawlings (Washington, D.C.: IVS, 1992), 1. The factors in the emergence of IVS and its implications for the Peace Churches will be discussed below.

118. J. Kenneth Kreider, 363. A specific record account of

Mennonites who served in IVS and where, has not been discovered by the author.

119. Ibid., 1. William T. Snyder, at the time assistant executive secretary of MCC, was secretary of IVS, and Harold Row of the BSC also served on the board. John S. Noffsinger, Brethren, became the first executive director January 1954. Kreider, 363.

120. See Kreider, chapter 17, "International Voluntary Services and Viet Nam Christian Service," for an extensive comprehensive account of the IVS program and the major projects including that in Vietnam.

121. Redekop, *The Pax Story*, 87. Jantzen had signed up for Germany, but when offered the Iraq opportunity eagerly opted for it.

122. Kreider, 287.

123. Ibid., 287.

124. Ibid. The conditions included the following: "Volunteers were expected to be Christian in faith and outlook, not motivated by humanitarian or secular purposes, and must show evidence of a personal commitment to Jesus Christ as Savior and Lord of their life," 288.

125. Kreider, 287-8.

126. Ibid., 288.

127. *MVS Newsletter*, January 1958, 3; see also *ME* 4, 1078. The short article lists MCC as the Mennonite participant, when in reality it was an MVS project.

128. Kreider, 288ff.

129. Wienss states that foreign service for German COs became "an option many years later."

130. *Mennonitesiche Geschichtsblaetter* (1967), 69. The Eirene office was housed in the MCC office in Kaiserslautern, Germany.

131. Kreider, 297. Wienss, personal letter, July 10, 2005. See also "*40 Jahre Eirene Chronik-1957-1997.*" The ecumenical nature of the program impacted the question of the leadership, so that "during the first five years, there were four different leaders," 296.

132. The right of conscientious objection in Germany has an astounding history. "The right to conscientious objection is more unequivocally specified in the Constitution of the Federal Republic of Germany than in any other country in the world. Article 4 of The Basic Law of 1949 states: 'No one shall be forced to do war service with arms against his conscience.'" The implementation of the law took place in 1956 with the formation of the "Bundeswehr" (National Army) and male conscription. The peace churches and their postwar activities in Germany, especially that of the Brethren, Mennonites, and Quakers provided extensive inspiration for the establishment of alternative service, *Zivildienst*. This is evidenced by the fact that "The charitable services of the Protestant and Catholic churches, the German Red Cross, and the German non-sectarian Welfare Organizations engaged about 60 percent of all the conscientious objectors serving in 1989." Charles D. Moskos and John Whiteclay Chambers II, *The New Conscientious Objection* (New York: Oxford University Press, 1993), 101. Thus the period from 1948 to 1956, when the foreign service organiza-

tions had largely done the physical and social reconstruction work in Germany, gave ample time for Germans to learn from, and adapt the practices of these foreign service organizations. The history of EIRENE is an obvious case in point.

133. Redekop, *The Pax Story*, 42.

134. Ibid., 44.

135. The reason for a one-year tenure was that MCC did not have any idea whether this kind of voluntary service in a foreign country would be recognized by Selective Service. Alternative service in foreign countries had not been recognized by the American SS system.

136. Redekop, 48. The time that elapsed between the time the idea was presented to the MCC and the sending of the first Pax unit to Europe was a scant seven months. This has to be one of the fastest mobilizations of personnel in Mennonite history.

137. See Redekop and Kreider for details of the negotiations and implemention of the alternative service work.

138. See Calvin Redekop, *The Pax Story*, 45 passim.

139. Harold S. Bender, "Mennonite Central Committee," *ME* 3, 607.

140. C. J. Dyck, "Mennonite Central Committee," *ME* 5, 561. Rationalization here refers to consciously creating a human structure that will most effectively use human efforts to serve a specific need or purpose. Max Weber has presented a classic analysis of this phenomenon.

141. See "Europe," by Harold S. Bender, for a comprehensive and incisive survey of the dynamics. "A serious twofold block to closer fellowship between the Dutch Mennonites and the remaining Mennonites of Europe was the differing theological and ecclesiastial development. . . . Liberal theology. . . ." *ME* 2, 260.

142. Ibid., 261. The relationship of European Mennonites is still tenuous though some rapproachment is emerging. One example is that the Dutch and German delegates to the Mennonite World Conference in the U.S. in 1948 did not talk with each other on the same ship to America. Paul Peachey was a witness to the tension on board ship and managed to get the two groups to at least meet together for a worship period. Paul Peachey personal interview, July 9, 2005. To his knowledge this incident has not been reported elsewhere.

143. This dynamic was a major tension in most of the camps which has not been discussed or examined.

144. As indicated in note above, there is little published evidence available on this topic. But it exists and needs to be dug out of the diaries of MCC workers and other such sources. The author, having spent three years among European Mennonites, has experienced this dynamic first hand.

145. Calvin Redekop, "Report of the Post Camp-Conference, Thomashof, August 28, 1950," 1. See Appendix "Thomashof" for full text.

146. In planning for the conference, the MCC voluntary service office had invited selected persons from the European Mennonite

countries to hear the reports and to report how they felt about the voluntary service program, how it had affected young people from their congregations, and how it might be improved. It was assumed that the experience of the invitees would affirm that the time had come for more direct involvement of Europeans in the program, so the MCC could become a "partner" rather than a "foreign" agent conducting the program.

147. Ibid., 1.

148. Calvin Redekop, "Development of Voluntary Service in Europe," Gospel Herald, Jan. 22, 1952, 88.

149. Calvin Redekop, "Report of V.S. and PAX Services to MCC Workers Conference," Ruedesheim, Sept. 27-30, 1950.

150. Calvin Redekop, "Meeting of the European V.S. Council, December 29-30, 1950," MCC Files. Present were Richard Hertzler and Otto Wiebe (Germany), Ernst Hege and Walter Mosiman (France), Samuel Gerber (Switzerland), Harold Buller, Paul Peachey, and Cal Redekop (MCC).

151. Ibid., 2.

152. Ibid.

153. Ibid.

154. Calvin Redekop, "MCC Activity Report," April 1951, 1.

155. Ibid. A Dutch representative was not present because the first person that was appointed by the Dutch did not accept the invitation. See Appendix V for the text of the Constitution.

156. See Appendix IV for transcript. "Provisorische Satzung des Mennonitischen Freiwilligen-Dienstes," April 10, 1951. Representatives present were Samuel Gerber (the teacher) Switzerland; Ernest Hege, France; Richard Hertzler, Germany; and Paul Peachey and Calvin Redekop, MCC staff. The Dutch were not able to find a suitable representative by the time of the meeting. The European representatives suggested that an European director would be most effective in soliciting responses from the youth, but attempts to locate such a person with experience were not successful for various reasons for a number of years.

157. Ibid., 1-2.

158. Calvin Redekop, "Report of V.S. and PAX Services to MCC Workers Conference, Ruedesheim September 27-30, 1951," 1.

159. Calvin Redekop, MCC Monthly Report, Nov. 1950.

160. The team was composed of Walter Bartel, a Prussian refugee; Eric Habegger, a Swiss youth who had been a VS volunteer; Milton Harder, director of the Espelkamp program; and Calvin Redekop, director of VS.

161. Bob Lee, "Mennonite Voluntary Service Work Camps," Annual Report, November 1951-Sept. 1952. Mimeo report, Frankfurt, 1952, 1.

162. Minutes, MFD, Espelkamp, April 9, 1951.

163. Ibid., 1.

164. Ibid., 1.

165. "MVS Survey Report," Fall 1951
166. Letter to Miller, Nov. 24, 1950.
167. Ibid., 2
168. This proposal, originally conceived as an international team, soon divided into two parts, the MVS Caravan as described here, and the Pax program, which took on its own character. MVS continued to contribute to the establishment of the Pax construction units but evolved along the concept of an international co-educational mobile team. The Pax program is expanded in Redekop, *The Pax Story*.
169. MVS Minutes, Basel, Feb. 16, 1952.
170. H. A. Fast letter to MVS council, Dec. 10, 1952.
171. The reasons the Europeans did not assume responsibility are not easily available and would require extensive research. I will offer some personal observations. One cause was the four Mennonite groups' lack of experience in cooperating with each other. The war and longstanding differing theological orientations had distanced the groups and hence made cooperation difficult. Thus MCC was able to elicit cooperation as an "objective arbiter," but when MCC began to withdraw, the old traditions reasserted themselves. Financial considerations were also involved, as indicated above. Further, the social and economic recovery of Europe decreased the importance of International Voluntary Service activities.
172. *MVS Newsletter*, Nov. 1954, 4.
173. Charles Moskos and John Whiteclay Chambers, eds., *The New Conscientious Objection: From Sacred to Secular Resistance* (New York: Oxford University Press, 1993), 221.
174. Footnote 89 above suggests that MVS may have played an important part in the recognition of conscientious objection to military service, especially in Germany, Holland, and Switzerland. This still needs to be investigated further. Considerable evidence has already been discovered to indicate that the Pax program in Germany was a major influence for the *Zivildienst* law. But it is not yet conclusive, especially what contribution international work camps made. More definitive research is necessary. Moskos and Chambers cited above make no reference to sources for the CO status, especially in Germany.
175. Kopp letter to O. O. Miller, June 24, 1955.
176. Ibid.
177. Dec. 7. Kopp letter to O. O. Miller.
178. Goering letter to MVS council, April 29, 1959.
179. "Position of the Youth Commission of the French Mennonite Church regarding cooperation with M.V.S.," Nov. 5, 1959. Translated from the German by author.
180. Ibid., 1.
181. Ibid., 2.
182. Reichert letter, Jan. 12, 1960.
183. Letter from Hans Jacob Galle to Abram Braun, May 17, 1961. Translated and summarized from the German by the author.
184. Ibid., 3.

185. *MVS Newsletter*, Christmas 1965.

186. *MVS Newsletter*, Sept. 1969.

187. Ibid., np (not paginated)

188. Ibid.

189. Ibid. Isert returned to Germany in 1970. "He will be directing the program of the Internationale Mennonite Organization [sic], the relief organization of European Mennonites," *MVS Newsletter*, Dec. 1970.

190. *MVS Newsletter*, Dec. 1969.

191. *MVS Newsletter*, March 1970. Jaap Rem, from the Netherlands, served as MVS director in Kaiserslautern in 1970-1971. He was followed by Hans Peter Bergtholdt.

192. *MVS Newsletter*, June 1970.

193. This article by Wienss includes verbatim plus abbreviated and condensed statements.

194. Ibid.

195. *MVS Newsletter*, Sept. 1970.

196. MVS Newsletter, March 1971. In this issue director Wienss presents an overview of, and personal reflection on the MVS program from its 1948 beginning to the present. The decision was made soon after Jon deVries was "elected chairman of the MVS Council [and] is replacing Raymond Kauffmann, of France." This reflected the fact that France had already withdrawn from the MVS council, *MVS Newsletter*, Dec. 1970.

197. Personal letter, Hans Joachim Wienss, May 16, 2005.

198. *Algemene Doopsgesinde Weekblad* 25, no. 1., Jan. 3, 1970.

199. Ibid.

200. *Algemene Doopsgezinde Weekblad*, March 6, 1971.

201. *Mennonitisches Jahrbuch*, 1972, 86.

202. See for example, *Mennonitisches Jahrbuch*, 1968.

203. The European help was directed to help recently arriving Germans from Russia, the so-called Aussliedler. "International Mennonite Organization," *ME* 5, 451-2.

204. Hans-Joachim Wienss, personal correspondence, July 10, 2005.

205. Interview, Barbara Hege Galle, dir. of CD, May 26, 2005. See "Zehn Jahre Christliche Dienste," for a very extensive description in *Bruecke*, 11/9, 1996, 132-133.

206. "International Mennonite Organization (IMO)," *ME* 5, 451.

207. Barbara Galle, op. cit.

208. *Christ Seul*, the French Mennonite Paper carries periodic announcements regarding such youth activities.

209. Galle, op. cit.

210. For a recent survey of fundamentalism and its influence on Mennonites, see "Fundamentalism" and "Evangelicalism," *ME* 5, 318-319 and 281-283.

211. I have expanded on this theory and theology of voluntary service in *Serving the Neighbor: The Alternative to Societal Collapse* (in preparation).

212. See Wilfred Unruh for his "Philosophy of MVS" (A-197-199). It reflects rather well many of the points made here. He states, "MVS may well be called the program of "disciples in overalls," 1-195.

213. "International Mennonite Organization (IMO)," *ME* 5, 451-452.

214. The material not yet been organized, and practically no analytical material has been produced regarding this issue from a European Mennonite perspective.

215. Hertzler, 649.

216. *Washington Post*, Friday 15, 2008, C5. Hunter uses archaic language, but obviously evil or good is not restricted to the male gender.

217. This axiom, variously expressed in leading world religions suggests its universality. It is strange that a deep comparison of this fact has never been done, at least to my knowledge. But see note 188.

218. Nevertheless, the sociological principle of "reciprocity" continues to lurk in scholarly thinking.

219. Kristin Goss, "Altruism," *Encyclopedia of Community*, 37.

220. This is not to imply that MVS had no problems, tensions, or failures. This dimension would demand a larger treatment and probably would not add much to what is already known about human group relations.

221. The MVS office received a vast number of unsolicited responses by campers expressing appreciation for the work camp experience.

222. Emphasis mine.

223. *MVS Newsletter*, Oct. 1958, 4.

224. *MVS Newsletter*, Jan. 1958, 3.

225. Ranked by number of volunteers.

BIBLIOGRAPHY

Algemene Doopsgezinde Weekblad, March 1971. Dutch Mennonite weekly church paper.

Bender, H. S. "Eirene." *Mennonite Encyclopedia* 4, 1078.

———"Europe." *Mennonite Encyclopedia* 2, 255-261.

———. "Voluntary Service." *Mennonite Encyclopedia* 4, 848-850.

Bruecke. IMO Publication, vol. 2, 1996.

Brunk, Emily. *Espelkamp.* Karlsruhe, Germany: Mennonite Central Committee, 1951.

Christ Seul. French Mennonite Conference Publication.

Daftary, Dolly and Amanda Moore McBride, "International Voluntary Service." http://atlas-conferences.com/c/a/m/k/87.htm

Der Mennonit. First published by Mennonite Central Committee, Basel, Switzerland.

Dick, William O. *Espelkamp on the German Frontier.* Austin, Tex.: private publication. 2005.

Ediger, Elmer. "Our Colleges and the Voluntary Service Program in the Present Crisis." *Proceedings of the Conferences on Mennonite Educational and Cultural Problems,* V, VIII, 1951, 54-61.

Fast. H A. Letter to MVS Council, December 10, 1952. MCC Files.

Foth, Peter J. "International Mennonite Organization." *Mennonite Encyclopedia* 5, 451-452.

Gingerich, Melvin. "Council of Mennonite and Affiliated Colleges. *Mennonite Encyclopedia* 1,. 722-23.

Goss, Kristrin. "Altruism." *Encyclopedia of Community* 5.1, 37-40.

Graber, Merlin. *Karlsschule.* Self published, 1983.

Harder, Milton. "Die Mennoniten at Espelkamp." In *Mennonite Life* (July 1952):109

Hertzler, Richard. "Mennonitscher Freiwillengendienst." *Mennonite Encyclopedia* 3, 649.

Het Algemeen Handelsblad. "Warga, Netherlands." June,1956.

Hildebrand, Gerhard, Calvin Redekop and Theo Glueck. *"Die Jugend auf der Weltkonferenz."* Mimeo, 1952.

Horst, Irvin B. *A Ministry of Goodwill.* Akron, Pa.: Mennonite Central Committee, 1950.

Kopp, LaMarr. *Report to the MVS Council.* April 1955.

Kreider, J. Kenneth. *A Cup of Cold Water: The Story of Brethren Service.* Elgin. Ill.: Brethren Press, 2001.

Lee, Robert. "Mennonite Voluntary Service Work Camps. Annual Report, November 1951-September 1952." MVS Office: Frankfurt, Germany, mimeo, 1952.

Luce, Donn. "Introduction." in Stuart Rawlings, eds. *The IVS Experience from Algeria to Vietnam.* Washington D.C.: IVS. 1992.

MCC Annual Meeting Minutes. Author files.

Mennonite Central Committee, Voluntary Service Letters. 1948ff. MVS Office: Frankfurt, Germany. Replaced by *MVS Newsletters.*

Mennonitisches Jahrbuch, German Mennonite Yearbook, various volumes.

Mennonitishe Geschichtsblaetter 5.69. 1967.

Mennonitishen Jugend: Nachrichten aus der Jugendarbeit." Transcript in author's files. 1952.

Moskos, Charles D. and John Whiteclay Chambers II. *The New Conscientious Objection.* New York: Oxford University Press, 1993.

MVS Newsletter. Published by MVS office at Frankfurt, beginning in May 1950 as vol. 21 to 1971. Formerly it was *Mennonite Central Committee Voluntary Service Newsletter,* begun in March, 1949.

Pax Newsletter. Orville Schmidt, ed. Published by Pax Publishing Committee, 2001-2006.

Peachey, Paul. *Voluntary Service Report.* Frankfurt: MCC, mimeo, 1949.

Penner, Harold. "Voluntary Service." *Mennonite Encyclopedia* 5, 917-918.

Redekop, Calvin W. "MCC Activity Report." April 1951. MCC Files.

———. "Report of V.S. and PAX Service to MCC Workers Conference, Ruedesheim, Sept. 27-30, 1951

———. "Meeting of the European V.S. Council December 29-30, 1950." MCC files.

———. "Development of Voluntary Service in Europe," *Gospel Herald,* Jan. 1952.

———."European Mennonite Voluntary Service." *Mennonite Life* (July 1952).

———. Letter to O. O. Miller. MCC files, 1950.

———. *The Pax Story: Service in the Name of Christ*. Telford, Pa.: Pandora Press U.S., 2001.

———. "Report of the Post-Camp Conference," Thomashof, mimeo, Aug. 28, 1950.

———. "Development of Voluntary Service in Europe. *Gospel Herald*, Jan. 1952.

Rush, Richard. *MVS Caravan, From my Personal Diary 1952*. Author's files.

Unruh, John D. *In the Name of Christ*. Scottdale, Pa. Herald Press, 1952.

Zeilsheim FFM Work Camp. Jan 2-Feb. 25. 1952. Author's files

THE INDEX

A
Aldworth, Sally 48,
Alternative Service ,77
  in Holland, 46, 77
  in Gemany, 91-92
  via IVS work camps, 54
American Mennonites, 64
  ignorance of Euroepan context, 65
  separating from European "brethren," 64-65
Arbeitskreis Internationale Gemeindschaftsdienste, 40

B
Backnang, 37
Bender, H. S., 65
Bergthold, Hanspeter, 50
Berlin, 47
Bertel, William, 40
Boyer, Paul
Braun, Abran, 82- 83
Brethren Service Commission, 46
  linked to Eirene, 56

C
Caravan, 33
  evolution of, 38,
expanded, 34
and Holland flood 43
  and Pax 58
  in Greece 45
  idea, 72
Camp leadership conference, 41
COs (Conscientious Objectors), 46
  and MVS, 46

Dutch, 46
Eirene, 56
German, 91-92
Ceresole, Pierre, 19, 20
Christian witness, 81
  lack of, 81-82
Christlicher Dienste, 91-92
Church of the Brethren, 46, 54
CMAC (Council of Mennonite and affiliated Colleges), 24
  sponsors of exchange and work, 24
College foreign exchange, 24,
  and work camps. 25
Construction units, 23
  relief function, 23
Coordination Committee for International Work Camps, 39-40
CPS (Civilian Public Service)
  origins of, 20
  problems with, 21

D
de Graff, Piet, 88
de Vries, Jan, 42, 50
  director of MVS, 43, 74-75
  skepticism among European Mennonites regarding MVS, 61
  French Mennonites, 79ff
  lack of spiritual guidance, 81
  national nature, 81
  regarding witness, 81
  Swiss, 82
Directors of MVS listed, 50
Dyck, Peter, 88

E

East German campers, 34
Easter Work Camps, 48-49
Ebersole, Myron, 42
Ediger, Elmer, 21
Eirene, 55
alternative service goals, 55
and German alternative
services, 56
and Dutch Mennonites, 90
links to MCC, BSC and
IFOR, 46
purposes of, 55
supportive of MVS, 90
Eisenbeis, Walter, 33
Esnes work camp, 19
Espelkamp, 26
camp project, 26
expansion of, 27
MVS meeting at, 67
Evangelical Church, Germany,
55
Evangelisches Hilfswerk, 26

F

Fast, H. A., 74
Fellowship of Reconciliation
(FOR), 55
Foth, Peter, 85
defends MVS, 86
Fieguth, Wolfgang, 70
Financing of MVS, 70-76
Frankfurt, 30
MVS office, 31, 70-72

Friends Ambulance Unit (FAU),
45, 76-77
Friesen, Hugo, 37
Fundamentalism/Evangelical-
ism, 92-93

G

Galle, Hans Jacob, 42, 82-83
Garber, Jacques, 42

Gerber, Samuel, 35, 42, 68-69
Germany
destruction of, 22
relief work in, 29
Glanville, Paul, 45
Glick, Theo, 42
Goering, Irvin, 50, 80
Germany, east, 45
Graber, C. L. 72
Greece, 45

H

Habegger, Daniel, 70
Harder, Milton, 25-27, 36
Harvey, Maureen, 48
Hege, Ernst, 35, 81
Hershey, General Lewis B, 57
Hertzler, Richard, 74, 98
Hirshy, Jean Jacques, 81
Historic Peace Churches, 20, 51,
54
Hochstettler, Roger, 44
Holland floods, 43, 45, 76
Huebert, Klaus, 91

I

International Voluntary Service
(IVS), 53, 54
providing alternative serv-
ice, 54
Isert, Joerg, 50, 83-84
Janzen, Curt, 37
Janzen, Carl, 54
Jost, Norma, 70

K

Kaiserslautern, 31,
Mennonitenhaus, 31
Kauffman, D.C. 45, 50, 80
Karlschule, 46-47
Kissel, Paul, 40
Klassen, C.F., 35, 72
Kloppenburg, Heinz, 54
Kopp, LaMarr, 40, 50

cooperate with Pax, 50
director travels, 44
MVS director, 74
Kreider, Robert, 22
Kreider, Kenneth, 55

L
Leadership, 70,
access to, 41
tensions, 74ff
conference, 32, 41
Lee, Bob, 37, 69

M
Mainz camp, 33-34
Marshall Plan, 58, 79
MCC (Mennonite Central Committee), 49
changing character, 64
defined, 63
early European relief, 30
in Frankfurt, 30
support of MVS, 22, 27, 41, 70
relations with European
Mennnites, 71
Menno Simons, 49
Mennonite Colleges, 23
international exchanges, 24
first European camp, 25
Mennonites, European, 90
and Dutch defense of MVS,
90-91
and German support of
MVS, 91
Mennonites, European and
MVS, 61
accepting MVS, 68-69
difference from NA Men-
nonites, 64-65
not happy with MVS, 80
concerns about MVS, 82
Mennonite Relief Committte, 23
Mennonite World Conference,
42

and German Mennonites, 91
and MVS future, 42
MVS council, 41
expansion, 42
founding of, 67
planning, 42
provison of office, 71
provisional constitution, 68
purposes of MVS, 84
Mennonite Voluntary Service
and Dutch support, 80
goals of, 69, 85
historical context, 64
meaning of, 98
peace witness of, 69
separation from PAX, 43
substance of, 95
structure of, 68
termination of, 89-90
reasons for, 93
transferral of, 91
to Dutch French, Ger-
mans, Swiss, 90
theology of, 89
Mennonitische Hilfswerk
Cristenflicht (MHC), 91
Miller, O. O., 57, 70, 80
Mistrust between American and
Europeans, 65
ameliorated by youth idealism, 65
Mosiman, Walter, 35
Nelson, Boyd, 29
Noe, Bim, 37, 50
Nieuwerkerk, 46

O
Offweilerhof, 36

P
Parris, Hubert,
Pax, 25, 37, 48, 54
relation to MVS, 56, 58
source of MVS, 72

Peachey, Paul, 30, 32
Penner, Rodney, 40
Power, 71
    unevenly divided, 71

Q
Quakers, 54
    cooperation with IVS, 54
    participation in IFOR, 55
Reconstruction, Europe, 23
    accelerating, 29
    increasing volunteers, 31
    role of CMAC, 30

R
Refugees, 34
Reichert, LaMarr, 40, 50
    director actions, 81-82

Rem, Jaap, 50, 85
Reunions, camp, 30, 83
Roff, Bill, 45
Ronneburg reunion, 30
Roupp, Alfred, 37
Rush, Richard, 37
Ruedesheim, 64

S
Schmidt, Orville, 40
Selective Service, 56
    and MVS, 57
    and Pax, 56, 72
    in Holland, 77
Showalter, Max, 81
Students' hunger, 33

T
Tensions regarding MVS, 76
    among European Mennon-
        ites, 95
    service versus witness, 92
    theology of MVS, 85-6, 89,
        92ff
Thomashof, 32, 65

Trocmé, Andre, 54
Truman, Harry, 57

U
Unruh, Benjamin, 35
UNESCO, 39, 44

V
Vacuum in Europe, 53
    Social, 53
    spiritual, 53
Vienna, 46, 47
Vietnam, 54
Visser t' Hooft, 54
Voluntary Service, 20
    emergence of, 21
    role of CPS, 20
    women's role, 21
    blessings and benefits of, 84-
        85

W
Waldensians, 32
Warga, Holland, 48
Wiens, Peter, 42
Wienss, Hans-Joachim, 31, 50,
        56, 83, 85
    and history of MVS, 87-90
Windishgarsten, 38
Witmarsum project, 49
Work camp motives, 65
    bridging American and Eu-
        ropean gaps, 65
    many benefits of, 84 ff.
    motives of, 65
    World Wars I and II, 64
    and Mennonites, 64

Y
Yoder, Marjorie, 70
Yoder, Sol, 37

Z
Zeilsheim, Pfalz, 37

THE AUTHOR

Calvin Wall Redekop was born on the Montana frontier in 1925 to Russian Mennonite parents, well indoctrinated in the ways Russian Mennonite families helped each other during the Stalinist era. After attending Goshen College, he volunteered for MCC service in Europe, especially Germany, heavily damaged during World War II. He was actively involved in organizing the PAX and Mennonite voluntary service programs. These experiences deeply influenced him regarding the importance of mutual aid and service in the functioning of a stable society.

He taught at several Mennonite colleges, retiring from Conrad Grebel College, Kitchener, Ontario, in 1990. He has written numerous books on topics including Mennonite community studies, power, environment, and service. He was also involved in a number of parallel church organizations such as Mennonite Economic Development Associates, international development in Paraguay and organizations promoting environmental sustainability, has lectured on these topics at various places, and has hosted numerous tours with Tourmagination.

He is married to Freda Pellman, is the father of three sons, and is a member of Park View Mennonite Church in Harrisonburg.

CPSIA information can be obtained at www.ICGtesting.com
Printed in the USA
266224BV00001B/13/P